Bud's Easy Research Paper Computer Manual

Alvin Baron

LAWRENCE HOUSE PUBLISHERS
Lawrence, New York

User's Input

Our goal is to improve this book continuously to make it easier for you to use. Here's your chance to give us your input.

Tell us:
- How you think the book can be improved.
- What you like about it.
- What you do not like.

Send comments with your name, address, and phone number to:
Research Director
Lawrence House Publishers
P.O. Box 329
Lawrence, NY 11559-0329

Thanks.

Bud's Easy Research Paper Computer Manual

ISBN 0-9609436-7-6

First Printing, September 1995
Second Printing, November 1995
Third Printing, February 1996

Trademarks

Trademarked names appear in this book. The publisher states that it used trademarked names only for editorial purposes and to the benefit of the trademark owner with no intention of infringing on those trademarks.

Every effort has been made to make this book as complete and accurate as possible, but no warranty or fitness is implied. The publisher assumes no responsibility for errors or omissions, or for damages resulting from the use of the information contained herein.

Published by Lawrence House Publishers
P.O. Box 329, Lawrence, New York 11559-0329.

Contents

How to Use This Book

Since 1977, with the publication of *Bud's Easy Term Paper Guide and Kit,* Lawrence House has been helping students with the writing of research papers. Two million of the Kits were sold as it went through nine editions over years. This book is an outgrowth of the original *Term Paper Kit,* much enlarged and brought up to date with the inclusion of the latest electronic and online research tools.

Now that the word processor has virtually eliminated the typewriter, many writers need help in making their word processing programs do what they want. This is especially true when confronted with an assignment to prepare a paper based on an unfamiliar model. That's why this book contains keystrokes for the four most popular word processing programs: Microsoft Word for DOS and Windows and WordPerfect for DOS and Windows—all in the latest versions and releases.

First, read **Chapter 1. BUD'S EASY TASK METHOD FOR TERM PAPERS, THESES, AND REPORTS** from beginning to end in order to get an overview of the planning, research methods, outlining and drafting which are necessary.

Second, decide, with your instructor, if required, which citation style you will use to document your paper. The four most frequently assigned styles, author-page, author-date, endnote, and footnote are each fully explained in separate chapters. The tab at the top of the page will help you locate the chapters quickly. Read the explanations for the style you will use.

Third, if you are a beginning computer user, locate your word processing program in Chapter 2. BASIC COMPUTER INSTRUCTIONS. Here you will find help with turning your computer on and starting your program. You will also find keystrokes for the basics such as centering text, underlining, saving and printing.

Fourth, within the chapter containing your citation style, locate the word processing program you will be using. Tabs along the edge of the pages will help you locate your program. Once you begin writing you will be assisted with all the keystrokes you need for formatting title, bibliography, and other special pages as well as specific instructions for page numbering, setting margins, and preparing tables.

Go to it and good luck with your project!

1 Bud's Easy Task Method for Research Papers, Theses, and Reports

INTRODUCTION

Research or term papers are assigned because writing them will enable you to:

- learn the skills to do exhaustive library research
- gather many facts and ideas on a specific subject
- hone your writing skills
- report accurately what you have discovered
- provide the reader with the sources you have read
- evaluate and select from among many ideas
- develop a hypothesis and defend it using research
- develop your thinking skills

The ability to do all of these tasks will prove valuable in many future school, college and work activities. While writing the research paper, or even the more comprehensive thesis, is a challenging and demanding job, you will find that you derive much satisfaction when you submit a carefully crafted paper to your instructor.

Bud's Easy Task Method breaks the seemingly monumental assignment into a series of relatively simple tasks and provides clear instructions which make it easy to succeed. If you follow the directions you will gain confidence as you complete each task knowing that you are moving along steadily. Remember the old adage, "The longest journey begins with a single step." Come along now and let's take the first step toward success.

TASK 1: GET STARTED

This task is simply to get moving. Procrastination is an unhealthful way of dealing with a job you don't like. Many people delay because they are afraid of failure. You may later ease your ego pangs over a D grade by claiming, "If I'd given it more time, I'd have gotten at least a B." Don't kid yourself! Be a responsible person. Get started now. Your instructor has given you directions about subjects, length, format, and due dates. Be sure you understand the assignment.

Divided into a series of tasks, the writing of a term paper is not as difficult as it first appears and it can even give you lots of satisfaction. You may even enjoy it. Let's go, right now! Continue reading all of Chapter 1 to get an overview of the whole job. Then go back and complete all of the separate Tasks.

TASK 2: SELECT A GENERAL TOPIC

This task is to select a general topic which will be refined to a thesis statement later. Study the **Topic Checklist** below. Then select your own general topic. Keep working until it passes all **Checklist** criteria. When you and your instructor are satisfied, go on to **Task 3**.

TOPIC CHECKLIST	
☐ **Not too broad**	"Preparations for D-Day" not "Causes and Results of World War II"
☐ **Not too narrow**	"Impact of Foreign Car Imports" not "The BMW Wheelcover"
☐ **Interesting to readers**	"Ocean Tides—Alternate Fuel" not the obvious "Should We Look For Other Fuels?"
☐ **Not too technical**	"Chemotherapy For Cancer" not "Carcinoma of the Right Central Pancreatic Duct" (unless you're a science major).
☐ **Scholarly**	"Influences on Coleridge's 'Kubla Khan' not "Rollerblades"
☐ **Interesting to you**	Opens a new challenging area to you.
☐ **Okay with instructor**	Meets subject, length, type, or other criteria.

My General Topic is _____

Time For Task 2: One Hour

TASK 3: SEARCH FOR INFORMATION

SEE IF THERE IS ENOUGH INFORMATION ON YOUR TOPIC

You want to include only information of the highest quality when writing a research paper. As you begin your search, use the **Source Quality Checklist** below to help you screen potential material.

SOURCE QUALITY CHECKLIST	
Primary Sources:	First hand material such as letters, documents, plays, novels, news stories. This is excellent material.
Secondary Sources:	Material written about primary sources, events, or ideas.
• Copyright date	Most recent unless historically significant.
• Author's reputation	Well-known in field, prolific, university scholar.
• Scholarship	Material footnoted, detailed, accurate. Not sensational, "low-brow," popular books or magazines.
• Relevance	Relates closely to topic.
• Bibliography	Extensive, scholarly sources.
• Objectivity	Clear point of view. Recognizes other ideas.

MANUAL CARD CATALOG SEARCH

If your library still has a card catalog, head for the subject catalog with a bunch of 3 × 5 index cards. Read all the catalog cards on your topic. Try to find at least five books on the topic. Complete a bibliography card for each book containing relevant information as shown in the sample on page 4. Assign each book a code number and write it on the upper right corner of the card in a circle. Be sure to copy accurately all publication information.

If there are at least five books on the topic, get them from the stacks and skim the tables of contents, indexes, chapter summaries and appendixes to see if each contains information on your topic. Write the page numbers on which you find material on the bibliography cards. Jot down a brief note describing what information is contained and how it is treated. Record the call number.

EASY TASK METHOD

SAMPLE BIBLIOGRAPHY CARD

Author ──────▶ Noyes, Russell   Your code number ──────▶ ③

Title ──────▶ William Wordsworth   Call number ──────▶ 821.7 / N

Publication city ──────▶ New York

Publisher ──────▶ Twayne Publishers, Inc.

Date ──────▶ 1971

Page numbers ──────▶ PP 68, 71, 105, 106

Your comments ──────▶ Good info on Tintern Abbey and nature themes.

ONLINE COMPUTER CATALOG SEARCH

If your library has a computerized catalog follow the instructions on the terminal. You will be able to find titles by entering the subject of your topic, the author or title. Some systems will present a list of subtopics. Select the one which most closely relates to your subject and a list of titles will appear. Select a title and bibliographic information, a brief summary and the call number will appear.

Some systems permit you to narrow your search more quickly by using the words, *and, not,* and *or.* For example, entering "trade barriers" *and* "Japan" will allow you to see all the works with information on both.

If a title looks promising, obtain a printout. The printout becomes a bibliography "card" although it will be on a sheet of paper. Write a circled code number in the upper right corner. Get the books from the stacks, skim the tables of contents and indexes to find information on your topic. Write the page numbers on which you find relevant data and jot a short note describing the material. Repeat the process until you have accumulated at least five "bibliography card" printouts of titles which fit your topic.

If full text printouts are available, print those which look good and put them aside for **Task 6. Gather Notes.**

MANUAL REFERENCE SECTION SEARCH

Head for the reference section. Search the *Reader's Guide to Periodical Literature,* encyclopedias, reference books, indexes related to your subject, and professional journals. Get the journals and reference books from the stacks and skim them to see if they are on target. Prepare 3 × 5 bibliography cards as described above.

ONLINE COMPUTER REFERENCE SEARCH

Many libraries are now switching from print reference indexes and ency-clopedias to CD-ROM set-ups, like *InfoTrac* which includes the *Reader's Guide to Periodical Literature* along with other indexes. Specialized indexes such as the *Education Index, Social Sciences Index, Psychological Abstracts,* the *Business Periodicals Index* and *Humanities Index* as well as those in other disciplines are also available on CD-ROM. *Grolier's Encyclopedia* and *U.S. History* are on CD-ROM with new titles being added regularly.

Libraries are rapidly integrating their entire collections of books, print and non-print reference materials into one online system. Some systems will enable you to search the catalogs of other public and university libraries. Ask your reference librarian for help.

Enter your general topic at the computer terminal. A list of subtopics will appear. Scroll through the list to find subtopics which match your general topic. Select one and a narrower list of articles will appear. Abstracts and even full texts are available on some CD-ROMs. If an entry looks good, obtain a printout and add them to your stack of bibliography cards. Repeat the process until you have printouts for several usable articles.

Read the abstracts or get the journals from the stacks and skim the articles to see if they are on target. Continue annotating the printouts with code num-bers and other data described above and add them to your collection of "bib-liography cards." See the sample computer printout bibliography "card" below.

If full text printouts are available, print those which look good and put them aside for **Task 6. Gather Notes.**

SAMPLE COMPUTER PRINTOUT BIBLIOGRAPHY "CARD"

```
InfoTrac * Magazine Index Plus ASA III *  (7)    ← Your
1992 -Jun 1995                                      code
                                                    number
      Heading: WORDSWORTH, WILLIAM
      3.   Criticism and creation. (literary
      criticism) (Column) by David Lawson v53
      The Humanist July-August '93 p23(2)
      69M5412
      ABSTRACT / TEXT / HEADINGS
      Excellent quote on humanism in       ← Your
      Wordsworth works.                       comments
```

INTERNET SEARCH

The Internet is a network of millions of interconnected computers which no one owns and which has no central facility. Finding information is difficult because in many ways the Internet started much like a library without central cataloging systems which are now being developed.

Most schools and colleges are accessing the Internet. If your school has a connection, the service will probably be free. Your system administrator will explain how you can log on. Many public libraries offer *Free-Net* service which provides Internet access. You may be a paying home subscriber to one of the computer services such as America Online, Prodigy, or Compuserve which provide access. Once connected, follow the screen instructions to navigate the Net for sources.

Detailed instructions for the Internet are beyond the scope of this book. You should check recent editions of Eric Braun's *The Internet Directory* or Ed Krol's *The Whole Internet: User's Guide and Catalog* for specifics. However, this brief overview of Internet operations will be helpful and at least give you some framework to begin posing questions to your system administrator or media specialist.

Internet Addresses

Internet addresses are similar to regular mail addresses, but look more complicated. They contain a series of names called *domains,* which are networks, separated by dots. From left to right, each domain or network is larger than the previous one. A series of top-level domains has been set up in the United States to identify the user's affiliation as follows:

com	—	**commercial and business**
edu	—	**educational institutions**
gov	—	**government institutions**
mil	—	**military institutions**
net	—	**network resources**
org	—	**other organizations**

For example, *starburst.uscolo.edu* means there is a sub-network called *starburst* connected to a network at the University of Southern Colorado and it is an educational institution. Rarely will you see addresses with more than five domains. A two letter country abbreviation usually ends the address when a country is designated. E-mail user's names are placed at the beginning and followed with the @ sign. Thus, *kwilliams@delaware.udel.edu* is the address of K. Williams at the University of Delaware.

The best way to get started with your search is to ask your media specialist or librarian for the latest editions of the *New Rider's Official Internet Yellow Pages, The Internet Complete Reference* by Harley Hahn and Rick Stout, and the *Directory of Electronic Journals, Newsletters, and Academic Discussion Groups* by Lisabeth A. King, Diane Kovacs, and others. Look for sources with information on your topic and copy the access addresses.

Newsgroup Search

Newsgroups provide subscribers an open discussion of ideas online in real time related to a specific field. There are now thousands of newsgroups and one for practically every subject. The easiest way to find your way is through a newsreader. Use one of the sources mentioned above to locate the newsgroup you want.

Much of the material in Newsgroups and Mailing lists is not of sufficient quality to use in your research. Always use the **Source Quality Checklist** before citing material from these sources as references.

Gopher Search

Gopher lets you search for resources using menus. It originated at the University of Minnesota which has a (you guessed it) for a mascot. Instead of accessing with the address of the domain, you select an entry in a gopher menu and like the human "gofers" of the world, Gopher goes for the material you want. Gopher is more like a regular library subject catalog and it will search the holdings of many libraries for your subject. The Internet does not have a standard for classification like the Dewey Decimal System or the Library of Congress, so searching may take some doing.

For example, if you want information on law, you might access via: *gopher fatty.law.cornell.edu* which is the Cornell Legal Information Institute of Cornell Law School.

See your system administrator, media specialist or librarian for help in using Gopher.

Wide Area Information Service (WAIS)

WAIS is best for searching for articles based on a specific subject. It differs from Gopher since it is more like a catalog for a private library devoted to a particular discipline. In Gopher you keep searching through menus until you locate what you want. In WAIS you name the subject and WAIS does the job and lists the relevant documents. It will even display them for you.

For example, if you want information on environmental safety, you can access via: *WAIS eshic.src* which is the Environmental Safety and Health Information Center.

The Internet now has a full collection of electronic texts and pieces of literature which can be retrieved with a new subset of WAIS called ALEX.

File Transfer Protocol (FTP)

FTP is used to transfer the millions of computer files including pictures, sounds, and books available on the Internet to your computer. Many sites are restricted to those who have an account to access and download the information. Today most public agencies allow free access to anyone using the word, *anonymous,* to log on and the user's Internet address as a password.

For example, if you want to download information on Iran, you can access via: *ftp tehran.stanford.edu;* login *anonymous.* This network is at Stanford University.

Archie Search

With so many computer files on public servers now online the job of locating and keeping track of them all requires a special program. Archie is a system which enables you to search for FTP programs, files, and data. Once you locate the ones you need, you can use *anonymous* FTP to transfer them to your computer.

World Wide Web (WWW)

As the Internet has grown, the need to organize its multiple resources has followed. The World Wide Web is the latest effort and it accomplishes its task by collecting many of the elements above under one umbrella organization. The Web is based on *hypertext* or *hypermedia* which is a technique for *linking* words to other sources. Several "browsers" or programs for searching the Internet are available including **www** and **Mosaic.**

When you enter the Web with one of the browsers, you see a "home page" which is a hypertext document. Each page contains words which are *links* to the other subjects. Web pages can hold text and graphics. By clicking or selecting the *links,* you open the next page with new information. There are an infinite number of paths to follow, narrowing the search for data. The Web is much more user friendly and flexible than Gopher.

URL or Uniform Resource Locator is the address for text or graphic on the Web. The letters HTTP for *HyperText Transfer Protocol* are always placed at the left of a URL when you are accessing a hypertext Web document. URL's for the Web frequently end in the letters *html* which stand for hypertext markup language.

For example, information on educational topics can be accessed via: *http://www.ed.gov* which is the address for documents in the U.S. Department of Education Online Library available on the Web.

CONTINUE COLLECTING INTERNET "BIBLIOGRAPHY CARDS"

Obtain printouts of any material that you download. Make sure that you assign a circled code number in the upper right corner and that you have all of the bibliographic information including the Internet source and address. Add the printouts to your stack of bibliography cards.

If full text printouts are available, print those which look good and put them aside for **Task 6. Gather Notes.**

GET AN OVERVIEW AND SEE HOW OTHERS TREATED THE TOPIC

After skimming several articles and books, you should have some idea of how others have dealt with your topic and what the major issues are. Look through the notes on the front of your bibliography cards or computer print-outs. What are the points of view? Are there many or a few? What are the major issues? Jot down a few ideas. Set the material aside for a day and let the information percolate in your mind.

DECIDE HOW YOU WILL DEAL WITH THE TOPIC

Now is the time to bring your own ideas into the project. Through your reading of sources, have you developed your own point of view? Do you agree or disagree with your sources? Has some new or original approach leaped into your mind? Could you apply the information in the sources in a new way? What do you think about this topic? Write down your thoughts. Let them flow. This is the most important part of the term paper project because it will lead directly to your writing the THESIS STATEMENT in **Task 4.**

Time For Task 3: 4–8 Hours

TASK 4: DEVELOP A THESIS STATEMENT

This task is to refine your ideas and develop a theme or thesis which can be "proved" or supported by your research. Read through the following list of **Thesis Approaches** to see which fits your thinking. You may want to re-read your bibliography cards or printouts once more. Note that the examples are all in declarative sentences which can be "proved."

THESIS APPROACHES

Chronology—	The rise of the Imagist Movement can be traced over a period of twenty years.
Procedure—	Five steps are required to produce liquid oxygen.
Cause/Effect—	Economic factors caused deterioration in Sino–Soviet relations from 1950–1979.
Problem—	Differing Moslem ideologies prevent Israeli–Palestinian peace.
Solution—	The energy crisis can be solved by solar, nuclear, and oceanic power.
Comparison—	Acupuncture is a better anaesthetic than malothane.

THESIS APPROACHES, continued

Similarity—	TV and motion picture writing are similar in several respects.
Difference—	Marriage rites differ among Far Eastern, Middle Eastern, and Western societies.
Relationship—	Hemingway's life influenced his work.
Analysis—	Three major issues are related to the crisis in Iran.
Literary Theme—	Romantic themes prevail in two major works of Wordsworth.
Pro—	Kennedy's handling of the Cuban missile crisis was a successful political move.
Con—	Four medical theories oppose radical mastectomy in breast cancer.
Category—	Several ethnic populations in America grew during the past ten years.

Now write your thesis statement in a declarative sentence. Identify which thesis approach you are using. Think the words, "I believe . . . " just before you write your thesis statement. This will insure that YOU and YOUR ideas are in the paper. Check your thesis against the following checklist.

THESIS CHECKLIST

My thesis statement is:
"(I believe) _____ **and it:**

      ☐ **uses the (select from list above) thesis approach.**
      ☐ **is not too broad.**
      ☐ **is not too narrow or technical unless required.**
      ☐ **can be proved with the material I have found.**
      ☐ **is scholarly.**
      ☐ **is OK with my instructor.**

If your thesis statement meets all the above criteria, go on to **TASK 5.** If not, return to **TASK 4** and write a new thesis statement.

Time For Task 4: 1–2 Hours

TASK 5: WRITE A PRELIMINARY TOPIC OUTLINE

This task helps your organize the information you have found to prove your thesis statement. The thesis approach will suggest the outline.

OUTLINING HINTS

1. Organize and classify ideas under major headings which support and prove the thesis statement. Do not include your introduction and conclusion in this outline. They will be written as part of **Task 9**.
2. Plan at least two subdivisions under each major heading. If you cannot, your outline is faulty. Subheads should also have at least two subdivisions.
3. The Preliminary Outline will tell you what information is lacking and send you back to the library to search for it. If you cannot find the material, revise your outline. Do not stretch or pad insufficient information.
4. Use the Harvard outline or the more modern decimal outline in which all information introduced by the same first numeral relates to the same major topic.

Harvard Outline	Decimal Outline
I.	1.
A.	1.2
B.	1.3
1.	1.3.1
2.	1.3.2
3.	1.3.3
a.	1.3.3.1
b.	1.3.3.2

5. Check your preliminary outline with your instructor if required.

SAMPLE OUTLINES

DIFFERENCE APPROACH

If you selected this approach, you have to identify the elements which differ and then show how they differ.

Thesis Statement: *Marriage rites differ among Far Eastern, Middle Eastern, and Western societies.*

1. **Marriage Rites in the Far East**
    1.1 **Vows**
    1.2 **Dowries**
    1.3 **Clothing**
    1.4 **Ceremonies**
2. **Marriage Rites in the Middle East**
    2.1 **Vows**
    2.2 **Etc.**

If you selected this approach, you must identify the themes and then show how they appear in the literary works.

Thesis Statement: *Romantic themes prevail in two major works of Wordsworth.*

1. **Romantic Themes**
   1.1 **Return to nature**
   1.2 **Sympathy with humble**
   1.3 **Escape from convention**
2. **Themes in Wordsworth's works**
   2.1 **"Tintern Abbey"**
       2.1.1 **Samples of return to nature**
       2.1.2 **Samples of sympathy with humble**
       2.1.3 **Etc.**
   2.2 **"Intimations of Immortality"**
       2.2.1 **Samples of return to nature**
       2.2.2 **Etc.**

Time for Task 5: 1–3 Hours

TASK 6: GATHER NOTES

This task is to take information from all of your sources and organize it in accordance with your Preliminary Outline. Go back to the library with your bibliography cards and/or computer printouts and your outline. Obtain the sources which relate to the first topic. Locate the pages which contain relevant material. Remember, you noted the page numbers on the bibliography cards or computer printouts in **Task 3**. Add any computer printouts you obtained from an Internet search. You are now ready to gather notes. This can be done by photocopying or in longhand. Read both methods to see which is better for you.

Whether you photocopy or use longhand, when you have finished this task put the completed notes aside for a day or so. Once again, let the material cook in your mind as the ideas you have just re-read, analyzed, and organized mix with your own.

PHOTOCOPY METHOD OF NOTE GATHERING

Most libraries charge only 10 or 15 cents per page. At that rate you can copy 100 pages for $10.00 or $15.00 which may be well worth it. Copy all the pages you need from each book or journal, making sure that you staple them together. On the upper left corner be sure to write the bibliography card code numbers and the original page numbers on the photocopies if they are not visible. Write the outline topic number and subject on the upper right corner of each sheet.

Use the same process for any computer printouts you obtained from Internet searches. Be sure each sheet has a code number which corresponds with a bibliography card and is labeled with the outline topic number.

Now carefully re-read each page with your outline to guide you. Decide which material fits each outline subtopic. Cut out separate paragraphs which match outline topics, again being sure to **write the bibliography card code numbers, page numbers, and outline topic numbers and subjects on each piece.** Continue this process until you have cut and labeled every paragraph. If there are some you cannot use, place these aside in a separate pile.

You may want to staple or paste each labeled paragraph on a 5×8 card or an 8×10 sheet of paper, but **be sure every paragraph is labeled with code number, page number and topic.** You should now have a pile of photocopied paragraphs or pages for each topic in your outline. If there are gaps, you may want to search for more information.

SAMPLE PHOTOCOPIED PARAGRAPH

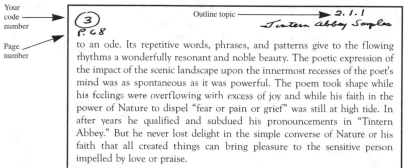

The page above is from Russell Noyes, *William Wordsworth* (New York: Twayne Publishers, Inc., 1971), P.68.

LONGHAND METHOD OF NOTE GATHERING

Take out your outline, bibliography cards and computer printouts. Obtain the books or articles which relate to the first topic. Locate the pages which contain relevant material. On a 5×8 card, **write the bibliography card code number and page number of the source in the upper left corner. Write the outline topic number and subject in the upper right corner.**

Now you must decide how you might use the material in the final paper. Detour temporarily now to the heading, **Assimilating the Note Material,** in **Task 8** which explains what to do.

When you have finished the explanation, summarize, paraphrase, or quote the information on your 5 × 8 cards. Use one side only and a separate card for each idea. Continue this process until you have prepared one of the three types of notes for each paragraph in your source material. **Be sure every card is labeled with code number, page number and topic.** You should now have piles for each topic in your outline. If there are gaps, you may want to search for more information.

Time for Task 6: 3–8 Hours

TASK 7: REVISE THE PRELIMINARY TOPIC OUTLINE AND CHANGE TO A SENTENCE OUTLINE

This task smooths out the Preliminary Topic Outline. Take a critical look at your work so far. Are the piles of notes of appropriate size or are there gaps? Too much for Topic 1 and not enough for Topic 3? Does the material now suggest a different approach? Would a Cause and Effect Approach be better than the Problem Approach you used? If the answer is "Yes" to any of these questions, your next task is to revise the preliminary outline. Rearrange your notes to match the new outline and change the outline topics in the upper right hand corners of the cards or printouts. Now look at the new piles to see that everything fits as it should.

Whether you are sticking with the original outline or you have revised, the next task is to change your Preliminary Topic Outline to a Sentence Outline in preparation for writing. Each topic should be transformed into a topic sentence around which your paragraphs will be constructed. Remember, a topic sentence is like a little thesis statement. Each sub-topic of the paper containing several paragraphs should "prove" or bear out its topic sentence.

CHANGE FROM TOPIC TO SENTENCE OUTLINE

Thesis Statement: *Romantic themes prevail in two major works of Wordsworth.*

Topic Outline	Sentence Outline
1. **Romantic Themes**	1. **Romanticism is associated with several themes which set it apart from neo-Classicism.**
1.1 **Return to nature**	1.1 **A return to nature and its beauty characterize the Romantic movement.**
1.2 **Sympathy with humble**	1.2 **The simplicity of the rustic life attracted many Romantic poets.**

Time For Task 7: 1–5 Hours

TASK 8: WRITE THE FIRST DRAFT

This task is to flesh out your outline. You will write paragraphs based on the topic sentences in the Sentence Outline. Decide, after studying the next section, how to use the researched material to support your ideas in the paragraphs. Write paragraphs by weaving your thoughts around the research notes, but be sure the major thesis and thrust of the paper is your own. Good writers do more than just cut and paste the ideas of others!

ASSIMILATING THE NOTE MATERIAL

Each researched idea you plan to use in your paper must be summarized, paraphrased, or quoted directly. Begin with the first topic in your outline. Locate a paragraph in a book or article which relates to the first topic. Study the directions below for summarizing, paraphrasing and quoting and decide which will support the topic best. If you are using the longhand method, paraphrase, summarize or quote each idea on a 5×8 card and arrange the cards according to your outline. If you are using the photocopy method, you must now decide which of the three techniques will be most effective and be prepared to use one of them for each source idea as you write your first draft. Note on each photocopy, "summarize," "paraphrase," or "quote." The samples below are based on the photocopied paragraph on page 13 from Russell Noyes' work.

SUMMARY: Author's ideas in your words in shortened version.

Directions: Read passage. Do not look at it again. Rewrite in your own words without your ideas or interpretation. Check for accuracy.

SAMPLE SUMMARY NOTE CARD

Your code number ➤

Page number ➤

Outline topic ➤

③
Page 68

2.1.1
"TINTERN ABBEY" SAMPLES

The rhythm and phrasing of "Tintern Abbey" reflects the strong feeling developed in Wordsworth as he reacted to Nature's landscapes. Later his belief in the power of nature was less fervent, although he always loved the simple joys it brought.

PARAPHRASE: Author's ideas in your words with no attempt to shorten.

Directions: Read passage. Do not look at it again. Rewrite in **your own words** without your ideas or interpretation, but do not shorten. Make author's ideas simpler. Check for accuracy.

SAMPLE PARAPHRASE NOTE CARD

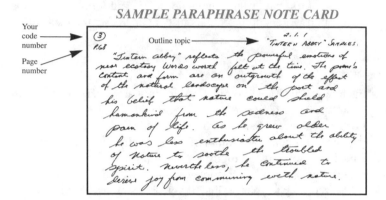

Your code number →

Page number →

③
P.68   Outline topic →   2.1.1
"TINTERN ABBEY" SAMPLES.

"Tintern Abbey" reflects the powerful emotions of near ecstasy Wordsworth felt at the time. The poem's content and form are an outgrowth of the effect of the natural landscape on the poet and his belief that nature could shield humankind from the sadness and pain of life. As he grew older he was less enthusiastic about the ability of nature to soothe the troubled spirit. Nevertheless, he continued to derive joy from communing with nature.

QUOTATION: Author's words exactly.

Directions: Using quotation marks, copy passage exactly including punctuation, underlining, etc. Even errors should be copied and followed with the Latin word, [sic], "thus," in brackets and underlined.

SAMPLE QUOTATION NOTE CARD

Your code number →

Page number →

③
P.68   Outline topic →   2.1.1
"TINTERN ABBEY" SAMPLES

"Its repetitive words, phrases and patterns give to the flowing rhythms a wonderfully resonant and noble beauty. The poetic expression of the impact of the scenic landscape upon the innermost recesses of the poet's mind was as spontaneous as it was powerful."

PLAGIARISM: Plagiarism is the improper use of another's ideas or language. Paraphrasing closely without giving credit or using original phrases or words without quotation marks are definitely examples of plagiarism. Academic and legal penalties are severe and can include a failing grade, expulsion, and even denial of college degrees. Be scholarly and honest.

BEGIN WRITING IN EARNEST

If you used the photocopy method, you can now transform your photo-copied paragraphs into summaries, paraphrases, or quotations. The easiest and perhaps fastest technique is to write your summaries, paraphrases and quotations directly from the photocopies and incorporate them into the first draft as you write. Be sure to cite the sources accurately.

If you used the longhand method, go back now to **Task 6: Longhand Method of Note Gathering,** paragraph 3 and continue through **Task 7** and **Task 8.** You now have a collection of note cards containing your sum-maries, paraphrases, and quotations. You can simply staple them directly to the pages of the first draft at the places where you want them to appear. On the other hand, you may insert them into your text at the appropriate points as you word process, type or write your paper.

Now begin to write in earnest. You can use a typewriter, word proces-sor, or even old-fashioned yellow legal pads. Double space on typewriter or word processor and skip lines in longhand to allow for revisions. Write quickly and forget style and grammar. Your goal is to get your thesis proved by getting your ideas and your research down on paper. Remember to put yourself into the paper. A good research paper is not a collection of quotes and paraphrases of other's ideas. The paper should reflect you.

Do not write the introduction or concluding pages at this time. Writ-ing in the third person only, begin with the first topic sentence from your sentence outline and write the paragraphs to "prove" it. Cite sources cor-rectly as you write. If you write in longhand, draw lines across the paper above and below the quoted, summarized, or paraphrased material to set it off.

Write the bibliography card code numbers and page numbers in the mar-gins near each paraphrase, summary or quote so you will be able to cite the source accurately in the final draft. Quotations should comprise no more than one fifth of the paper. Plan to have no more than four citations per page.

Write the transitional sentences and paragraphs which tie the researched material together. Point out disagreements and problems.

If you are word processing, be sure to save your writing to the hard disk and to your own floppy disk every fifteen minutes. Work straight through to the end without stopping and put your paper aside for a day when you finish.

Time for Task 8: 4–8 Hours

TASK 9: REVISE THE FIRST DRAFT

Now reread your paper for content. Note errors and ideas for changes in the margins. Rewrite, cross-out, and add between the lines. Revise on the word processor if you are using one.

Use the **Content Checklist** below to be sure your paper is okay. Ask someone else to read your paper to see if it meets all the criteria.

CONTENT CHECKLIST	
☐ Paper follows outline.	☐ Sources are cited.
☐ Material is logically developed.	☐ Potential plagiarism checked.
☐ Thesis is clearly stated.	☐ Your ideas are apparent.
☐ Thesis is proved.	

Write the introduction. Tell why you wrote the paper. Describe the positions others have taken on the subject. State your thesis and tell how you approached the topic. Explain the major points in the paper. Discuss the reasons why others should be interested in the topic.

Write the conclusion. Restate the thesis. Summarize the ideas and arguments presented. Explain your conclusions. Discuss leads to further investigation. Tell why you think your paper is interesting and worthwhile.

Reread the paper for grammar and style. Word processing programs like Grammatik and Spellguard are helpful. Electronic typewriters with dictionaries can also be used. Make corrections as needed.

GRAMMAR AND STYLE CHECKLIST	
☐ Clear topic sentences in all paragraphs.	☐ No dangling participles.
☐ Sentences support topic sentences.	☐ Strong verbs and nouns.
☐ No fragments or run-ons.	☐ Language smooth and fluent.
☐ Sentence openings and lengths vary.	☐ Good transitions between paragraphs.
☐ Same tense used throughout.	☐ Short quotes woven into text.
☐ Subjects and verbs agree.	☐ Spelling correct.
	☐ Only third person used.

Time For Task 9: 2–6 Hours

TASK 10: TYPE THE FINAL DRAFT

Most colleges, schools and universities adopt one of several scholarly styles for writing research papers. The most frequently used are *A Manual for Writers of Term Papers, Theses, and Dissertations,* 5th ed. which is based on the *Chicago Manual of Style;* the *MLA Handbook for Writers of Research Papers,* 4th ed.; and the *Publication Manual of the American Psychological Association,* 4th ed.

CITING SOURCES—CHOOSE ONE METHOD

Author-Date or Author-Page or Endnote or Footnote

As mentioned before, you must tell your reader whose ideas, besides your own, you have included in the paper. By using a citation, you identify the source including the author, title, and publication information. Your readers will then be able to locate the original material. The three stylebooks suggest different methods of citing sources. Traditionally, footnotes have been the most popular technique, but endnotes and now author-page and author-date citations which appear in parentheses in the body of the paper are widely used. Formats for bibliographic information also vary according to the stylebook.

Decide with your instructor which of the citation styles you will use. Before proceeding, study carefully the specific instructions for that style which you will find in the following pages.

FINAL DETAILS

All formal papers must be in typewritten form. Today's student may choose from among several word processing programs as well as manual, electric, and electronic typewriters. This book contains instructions for formatting papers using WordPerfect and Microsoft Word in both Windows and DOS environments because they are among the most popular programs.

Use 8½ × 11″ high quality, non-erasable paper. Pica, elite or other standard typefaces in black ink are acceptable. If you are wordprocessing, your final draft must be done on a letter quality printer only. Daisy wheel printers which print a series of dots are not acceptable.

Rewrite the paper including all revisions, deletions, and additions. Follow the instructions in this book for the style and word processing program you have selected. Pay careful attention to title pages, margins, pagination, citation technique, and especially the method of preparing the bibliography. Styles vary with regard to handling quotations, too.

After typing or printing on a word processor, proofread carefully again for omitted words, punctuation, and spelling errors. You should now have a paper which you can present to your instructor with pride. Congratulations! Hope it earns an A plus! You deserve it.

Time For Task 10: 4–8 Hours

2 Basic Computer Instructions

WordPerfect-DOS & Windows
Microsoft Word-DOS & Windows

COMPUTER BASICS

The following pages will help if you are unfamiliar with basic computer operations. Simplified explanations for WordPerfect and Microsoft Word in both DOS and Windows environments are given for opening, saving, and printing as well as other common procedures.

Locate the program you are using in DOS or Windows and follow the instructions.

WORDPERFECT FOR DOS 4.2–6.0

OPENING WORDPERFECT

1. Type at the C:\> prompt, WP. The WordPerfect screen will appear.
2. If this is the first entry of your paper, just begin typing.
3. If you have already saved your paper with a file name, press Shift+F10. The message, "Document to be retrieved:" will appear in the lower left corner. (In **WordPerfect 6.0** the Open Document dialog box will appear.)
4. Type in the filename and press Enter. Your document will appear.

UNDERLINING

WordPerfect 6.0

1. Move cursor to first character to be underlined.

2. Press F12 to turn Block on and then move cursor to end.
3. Press Ctrl+U. The entire block will be underlined.

or

1. Press Ctrl+U and type words to be underlined.
2. Press Ctrl+U again to end underlining.

WordPerfect 4.2–5.1

1. Move cursor to first character to be underlined.
2. Press F12 to turn Block on and then move cursor to end.
3. Press F8. The entire block will be underlined.

or

1. Press F8 and type the words to be underlined.
2. Press F8 again to end underlining.

CENTERING

1 Move cursor to first character to be centered.
2. Press F12 to turn Block on and move cursor to end.
3. Press Shift+F6 in **6.0** and add Y in **4.2–5.1.**

or

3. Press Shift+F6 and type text to be centered.
4. Press Enter to return cursor to left margin.

SAVING

Every fifteen minutes you should save your paper to avert disaster.

1. Press F10 and the Save Dialog box appears. (Document to be saved prompt appears in **WordPerfect 4.2–5.1**).
2. Type a filename of no more than eight characters.
3. Press Enter. Your file name appears at lower left to show that it has been saved.
4. Every fifteen minutes, press Ctrl+F12 and your work will be saved to the disk. (Press F10, Enter and Y in **WordPerfect 4.2–5.1**).

PRINTING

1. Press Shift+F7 and the Print menu appears.
2. Press Enter. (Press 1 in **WordPerfect 4.2–5.1**).
3. Select from the Print menu for other options.

QUITTING WORDPERFECT

Press F7, Y to save your work, Enter, Y to update to disk, and Y to exit WordPerfect.

MICROSOFT WORD FOR DOS 5.0–6.0

OPENING MICROSOFT WORD

1. Type at the C:\> prompt, cd\Word5 or Word and press Enter. Word5 or Word appears at the C:\> prompt.
2. Type Word and press Enter. A new, unnamed document window appears.

UNDERLINING

Microsoft Word 6.0

1. Move the cursor to the first word you wish to underline.
2. Press F8. Each time you press F8 another word will be highlighted.
3. Press Ctrl+U.
4. Press Ctrl+spacebar twice to stop underlining.

Microsoft Word 5.0

1. Move the cursor to the first word you wish to underline.
2. Press F6, then F8. Each time you press F8 another word will be highlighted.
3. Press Alt+U.
4. Press Alt+space bar twice to remove underlining.

CENTERING

Microsoft Word 6.0

1. Move the cursor to the first word you wish to center.
2. Press F8. Each time you press F8 another word will be highlighted.
3. Press Ctrl+C. The entire sequence will center.
4. Press Ctrl+L to move cursor to the left margin.

Microsoft Word 5.0

1. Move the cursor to the first word you wish to center.
2. Press F6, then F8. Each time you press F8 another word will be highlighted.
3. Press Alt+C. The entire sequence will center.
4. Press Alt+L to move cursor to the left margin.

SAVING

Every fifteen minutes you should save your paper to avert disaster.

Microsoft Word 6.0

1. Choose Save As from the File Menu. The Save As dialog box appears with the cursor in the File Name text box.
2. Type a file name of no more than eight characters if this is the first time you are saving and choose OK. The Summary dialog box appears.
3. Complete the entries and choose OK.
4. After you have saved once, press Shift+F12 and Microsoft Word will save the document with the file name you chose.

It is a good idea to save to your own floppy disk in case of a hard drive failure.

1. Insert a formatted floppy disk in the A drive.
2. Choose the A drive from the Save As dialog box and press Enter.

Microsoft Word 5.0

1. Press Esc, T for Transfer, S for Save. Word asks for a filename. If this is the first time you are saving, at the C: prompt type in a filename containing no more than eight characters.
2. Press Enter and Esc to return to your writing.

It is a good idea to save to your own floppy disk in case of a hard drive failure.

1. Insert a formatted floppy disk in the A: drive.
2. Press Esc,T and S. At the prompt, type A:and your filename.
3. Press Enter and Esc.

PRINTING

Microsoft Word 6.0

1. Choose Print from the File Menu. The Print dialog box appears.
2. Select number of Copies, Page Range, or selected Pages and Choose Print and OK.

Microsoft Word 5.0

1. Press Esc, P for Print, O for Options.
2. Select the printing options you desire and press Enter.
3. Press Esc, P for Print and P again for Printer.

QUITTING MICROSOFT WORD

Microsoft Word 6.0

1. Choose Exit from the File Menu
2. Choose Yes to save changes.

Microsoft Word 5.0

1. Press Esc and Q for Quit.

WORDPERFECT FOR WINDOWS 5.2–6.0

OPENING WORDPERFECT FOR WINDOWS

1. Type at the C:\> WIN and press Enter. Program Manager window appears.
2. The mouse pointer assumes several shapes depending on the situation. Now it appears as an arrow. Several mouse terms will be used in these instructions. Point means move the mouse pointer to a specific place. Click means press and release. Double click means click twice. Drag means hold down mouse button, move the pointer to a place and release.
3. Double click on the WordPerfect icon in Program Manager. The WordPerfect window appears.
4. Double click on the WPWin icon. WordPerfect Document1 - Unmodified window appears.
5. The cursor, a flashing vertical bar appears at the top left of the screen. This shows where you are in the document. You can move the cursor through text with the space bar, arrow, Enter, Home, End, Page Up,

Page Down keys as well as by moving the I-beam, another form the mouse assumes, with the mouse and clicking.

UNDERLINING

WP 5.2

1. Select text to be underlined by dragging across the words and releasing.
2. Click on Font and Underline in the Menu Bar. Selected words will be underlined.
3. Click anywhere and the highlighting will disappear.
4. Move the cursor to the spot where you will resume typing and click.

WP 6.0

1. Select text
2. Click the U button in the Power Bar
3. Click anywhere on the screen to end selection.
4. Click the U button again to turn off underlining

CENTERING

WP 5.2

1. Place the cursor at the left margin.
2. Press Shift+F7 The cursor will shift to the center of the line.
3. Type the words you want to center.
4. Press Enter to turn off centering.

or

WP 5.2 and WP 6.0

1. Click on the Justification button in the Ruler.
2. Drag down to Center and release.

SAVING

Every fifteen minutes you should save your paper to avert disaster.

1. Click on File and Save in the Menu Bar after typing one page of text. The Save As dialog box appears.
2. Type a file name consisting of no more than 8 characters.
3. Click on Save or OK. Repeat this process every 15 minutes by pressing Save in the Button Bar.

WordPerfect can protect you from losing any text with its automatic timed backup feature.

1. Click on File, Preferences, and Backup in the Menu Bar. A Backup dialog box appears.
2. Click on Timed Document Backup and an X appears. Use the arrows to set the number of minutes between backups.
3. Click on OK.

PRINTING

1. Click on File and Print in the Menu Bar. The Print dialog box appears.
2. Click on the Options you desire. Use the settings to select the number of copies.
3. Click on the Document Settings you wish.
4. Click on Print.

QUITTING WORDPERFECT FOR WINDOWS

1. Click on File and Exit. A WordPerfect dialog box will appear with the prompt *? Save changes to c:\wpwin\filename.*
2. Click on Yes to save the document. The Program Manager window appears.
3. Double click on upper right button. The Exit Windows dialog box appears. Click on OK.

MICROSOFT WORD FOR WINDOWS 5.2–6.0

OPENING MICROSOFT WORD FOR WINDOWS

1. Type at the C:\> prompt, WIN and press Enter. The Program Manager window appears.
2. The mouse pointer or cursor assumes several shapes depending on the situation. It may appear as an arrow or an I beam. Several mouse terms will be used in these instructions. Click means press and release. Double click means click two times. Drag means hold down mouse button and move the pointer to a place on the screen and release. Point means move the pointer to a specific place on the screen.
3. Double click on the Word for Windows icon in Program Manager. The Word for Windows box appears.
4. Double click on the Microsoft Word icon. A Microsoft Word Document1 window appears. The cursor, a flashing vertical bar appears at the top left of the screen. This shows were you are in the document.

You can move the cursor through text with the space bar, arrow, Enter, Home, End, Page Up, and Page Down keys as well as by moving the I beam with the mouse and clicking.

UNDERLINING

1. Select text to be underlined by dragging across the words and releasing.
2. Click on the _U_ button in Toolbar.

or

1. Press Ctrl+U to underline and Ctrl+Spacebar twice to stop underlining.

CENTERING

1. Move the cursor to a new line.
2. Press Ctrl+E. The cursor will move to the center of the page.
3. Type the words you want centered.
4. If the words are already typed, select the words.
5. Press Ctrl+E.
6. Press Ctrl+L to return cursor to the left margin.

or

1. Select text and click on the centering button in the Toolbar just to the right of the B, _I_, _U_ buttons.
2. Click on the flush left button to stop centering.

SAVING

Every fifteen minutes you should save your paper to avert disaster.

1. Click on File and Save in the Menu Bar after typing one page. The Save dialog box appears.
2. Type the name of your document in the File Name box using no more than eight characters.
3. Click on OK. The name of your document appears in the Save As list. Every ten or fifteen minutes click on the Save button in the Tool Bar. It is the third button on the left side and looks like a miniature floppy disk.

In addition, it is a good idea to save your work to a floppy disk which you should keep in a separate place.

1. Insert a formatted disk in the A drive.
2. Click on File and Save As in the Menu Bar.
3. Click on the Drives drop down list and choose A:

4. Enter your file name in the File Name text box.

5. Click on OK.

PRINTING

1. Click on the Print button in the Toolbar. It looks like a miniature printer and can be found on the right side of the bar next to the ABC spell check button. Printing will begin if your printer is loaded and ready.

or

1. Click on File and Print in the Menu Bar. The Print dialog box appears.

2. Click the up or down arrows in the Copies box for the number of copies you want.

3. Click on the appropriate spot in the range box. For specific pages, click on Pages and type the page numbers you want to print.

4. Click on OK.

QUITTING WORD FOR WINDOWS

1. Click on File and Exit in the Menu Bar. The Word for Windows box appears.

2. Double click on the upper left button. Program Manager appears.

3. Double click on the upper left button. Exit Windows box appears.

4. Click on OK.

3 Author-Page Citation

MLA Handbook for Writers of Research Papers, 4th Ed., 1995

PARENTHETICAL AUTHOR-PAGE CITATION TECHNIQUE

This is an easy way to cite sources. The author's last name and the specific page number of the work where the material can be found are placed in parentheses in the text. A little practice may be necessary to insert the references and keep the writing fluent. Samples of common parenthetical references are below.

A bibliography called Works Cited, printed on a separate page at the end of the paper, provides complete publication information for each of the sources cited.

BOOK—SINGLE AUTHOR

Insert the last name of the of the author and page number(s) in parentheses in the text. It is easy to place the parenthesis at the end of the sentence.

```
    This concept has been reported earlier (Baron
148).
```

or

If author's name appears in text, insert only the page number in parentheses.

```
    Baron reported this concept (148).
```

BOOK—WHOLE WORK

Author's name and title of whole work may appear in text without parentheses.

```
    Shakespeare's Hamlet has been called his most
enigmatic tragedy.
```

PARENTHETICAL AUTHOR-PAGE CITATION TECHNIQUE

BOOK—MULTIPLE AUTHORS

Place multiple authors' names and page number(s) in parentheses.

An opposing idea has also been explored (Brown and Roberts 179-81).

or

If multiple authors' names appear in the text, insert only the page number(s) in parentheses.

Brown and Roberts (179-81) explored an opposing idea.

MULTIPLE WORKS BY SAME AUTHOR

If two or more works by same author will be cited, insert author's name, shortened title, and page numbers in parentheses.

Most humans experience depression, often for reasons unknown to them (Rogers, Psychology 171-73).

or

If two or more works by same author will be cited and author's name and title appear in text, insert only the page number(s) in parentheses.

In Psychology and Modern Man, Rogers explains that most humans experience depression, often for reasons unknown to them (171-73).

or

If two or more works by same author will be cited and author's name appears in text, insert the title and page number in parentheses.

Rogers explains that most humans experience depression, often for reasons unknown to them (Psychology and Modern Man 171-73).

MULTI-VOLUME WORK

Insert author's name and volume number followed by a colon, space and page number(s) in parentheses.

Economic policy should provide for maintenance of full employment (Johnson 2: 273).

PARENTHETICAL AUTHOR-PAGE CITATION TECHNIQUE

or

If author's name and volume appear in the text, place only the page number(s) in parentheses.

In volume 2, Johnson suggests that economic policy should provide for maintenance of full employment (273).

or

If the whole volume is cited without reference to pages, insert the author's name and abbreviation for volume in the parentheses.

Economic policy should provide for maintenance of full employment (Johnson, vol. 2).

CORPORATE OR GOVERNMENT PUBLICATIONS
Insert corporate author in text and place page number(s) in parentheses.

In 1984 the United States Department of Defense issued a report denying activity in Paraguay (31).

or

Insert corporate author and page number(s) in parentheses.

A recent report denies any United States activity in Paraguay (United States Department of Defense 31).

MAGAZINE OR JOURNAL ARTICLES
Use same techniques as for books.

NOVELS
Insert the page number(s) followed by a semicolon and the chapter number.

The opening words of <u>Moby Dick</u>, "Call me Ishmael," quickly identify the narrator (1; ch.1).

PLAYS
Insert act, scene, line(s) separated by periods in parentheses but omit page numbers.

The queen finds relief in believing her son, Hamlet mad (III. iv. 105).

PARENTHETICAL AUTHOR-PAGE CITATION TECHNIQUE

UNSIGNED WORK

Insert title or abbreviation and page number(s) in parentheses

The <u>New Yorker</u> reprinted a story on country dining ("Country Inns and Byways" 213).

or

Insert title of whole unsigned work in parentheses

The spectrum is visible when white light is sent through a prism ("Color and Light").

QUOTATIONS

Prose

Quotations of four lines or less are not set off from the text but are placed within double quotation marks. Use single quotation marks for quotations within a short quotation.

For longer quotations, use a comma or colon after the last word of text, double space and type the quotation with no quotation marks. Indent ten spaces from left margin and double space quote. If two or more paragraphs are quoted one after another, indent the first line of each paragraph three more spaces. Use double quotation marks for quotations within a long quotation.

Poetry

Poetry of three lines or less is placed in double quotation marks within the text. Separate lines of poetry which appear in a single line of text by a slash (/) with a space before and after the slash.

For longer poems, use same procedure as for prose. Longer lines may be indented fewer spaces to improve balance.

GENERAL RULES

Periods and commas are placed inside quotation marks. Question marks and exclamation marks not originally in the quotation go outside the quotation marks. Words omitted (ellipses) are shown by three periods with a space between each and a space before the first period and after the last. If a parenthetical reference ends a quoted line, place the period after the reference.

WORKS CITED—BIBLIOGRAPHY

The bibliography is called Works Cited in MLA style. The short parenthetical references in your text lead the reader to the list of sources found on the page following the last line of your paper. Entries are alphabetized letter by letter by author's last name, association or title if author's name is not known. Entries are shown single-spaced here to conserve space in this book, **but they must be double-spaced in your paper.**

AUTHOR-PAGE CITATION

MLA WORKS CITED SAMPLES

PRINT SOURCES

BOOKS

BOOK—NO NAMED AUTHOR

Handbook of Pre-Columbian Art. New York: Johnson,
    1988.

BOOK—ONE AUTHOR

Gershman, Herbert S. The Surrealist Revolution in
    France. Ann Arbor: U of Michigan P, 1994.

BOOK—MULTIPLE AUTHORS

Raffer, Bernard C., Richard Friedman, and Robert A.
    Baron. New York in Crisis. New York: Harper, 1986.

BOOK—SAME AUTHOR(S)—
USE 3 HYPHENS AFTER FIRST ENTRY

---. A Study of Life. New York: Norton, 1993.

BOOK—EDITED

Melville, Herman. Moby Dick. Ed. J.P. Small. Boston:
    Houghton, 1973.

BOOK—TRANSLATION

Maurois, Andre. Lelia. Trans. Gerard Hopkins. New
    York: Harper, 1954.

BOOK—CORPORATE AUTHOR

National Policy Association. Welfare Reform. New York:
    McGraw, 1992.

MULTIVOLUME WORK—CITING ONE VOLUME ONLY

Smith, Richard K. A History of Religion in the United
    States. Vol. 3. Chicago: U of Chicago, 1993.

MULTIVOLUME WORK—CITING MORE THAN ONE VOLUME

Smith, Richard K. A History of Religion in the United
    States. 4 vols. Chicago: U of Chicago, 1993.

GOVERNMENT PUBLICATION

United States. Dept. of Labor. Labor Relations in the
    Steel Industry. Washington: GPO, 1994.

MLA WORKS CITED SAMPLES

DISSERTATION—UNPUBLISHED

Samson, Robert. "The Influence of Economic Deprivation
    on Academic Achievement." Diss. New York U, 1985.

DISSERTATION—PUBLISHED BY UNIVERSITY MICROFILMS

Garon, Lois. Socialist Ideas in the Works of Emile Zola.
    Diss. Brown U, 1992. Ann Arbor: UMI, 1993. 921437.

POEMS, ESSAYS, SHORT STORIES, PLAYS IN ANTHOLOGIES

Poe, Edgar Allan. "The Raven." Great American Poetry.
    Ed. Richard Johnson. New York: McGraw, 1978. 38-40.

PERIODICALS AND ARTICLES

ARTICLE IN REFERENCE BOOK—UNSIGNED

"DNA." Encylopedia Americana. 1994 ed.

ARTICLE IN REFERENCE BOOK—SIGNED

Smith, Richard. "Color and Light." Encyclopedia Brit-
    tanica. 1994 ed.

NEWSPAPER ARTICLE—SIGNED

May, Clifford. "Religious Frictions Heat Up in Rwanda."
    New York Times 12 Aug. 1994, late ed.: A1.

MAGAZINE ARTICLE—UNSIGNED

"Making of a Candidate for President." Time 20 July
    1984: 40-42.

MAGAZINE ARTICLE—SIGNED

Kuhn, Susan. "A New Stock Play in Saving and Loans."
    Fortune 15 May 1995: 67-72.

EDITORIAL—UNSIGNED

"China's Conscience." Editorial. New York Times 19 May
    1995, late ed.: A22.

EDITORIAL—SIGNED

Brownhurst, Marshall S. "Rush to Judgement." Editorial.
    Wall Street Journal 5 June 1995: A15.

ABSTRACT IN ABSTRACTS JOURNAL

Frischman, Josephine K. "Analysis of Bias in Selecting
    Test Times." Journal of Experimental Psychology 98
    (1992): 325-331. Psychological Abstracts 80
    (1993): item 7321.

MLA WORKS CITED SAMPLES

ARTICLE IN LOOSELEAF COLLECTION
SOCIAL ISSUES RESOURCES SERIES-SIRS

Cruver, Philip C. "Lighting the 21st Century." <u>Futurist</u>
    Mar. 1990: 29-34. <u>Energy</u>. Ed. Eleanor Goldstein.
    Vol. 4. Boca Raton: SIRS, 1991. Art. 84.

ARTICLE IN MICROFICHE COLLECTION—NEWSBANK

Chieper, Randy. "Welfare Reform Debates." <u>New York</u>
    <u>Times</u> 20 Apr. 1994, late ed.: A12. <u>Newsbank:</u>
    <u>Welfare and Social Problems</u> 17 (1994): fiche 2,
    grids A9-13.

REVIEW OF BOOK, FILM, PERFORMANCE

Include authors, directors, conductors, performers, others as pertinent.

Maslin, Janet. "New Challenges for the Caped Crusader."
    Rev. of <u>Batman Forever</u>, dir. Joel Schumacher. <u>New</u>
    <u>York Times</u> 16 June 1995, late ed.: C1.

ARTICLE
SIGNED IN JOURNAL WHICH USES ISSUE NUMBERS

Brogdan, Robert. "Religious Freedom and School Holi-
    days." <u>Phi Delta Kappan</u> 68 (1984): 700-702.

ARTICLE
SIGNED IN JOURNAL WHICH PAGES ISSUES SEPARATELY

Jones, Mary. "Urban Poetry." <u>American Review</u> 13.2
    (1987): 66-73.

NON-PRINT SOURCES

TELEVISION OR RADIO PROGRAM

Include show title, program or series title, pertinent actors, directors, producers, network, call letters and city, date.

"Pollution in the Desert." Narr. Mike Wallace. Prod.
    Jock Fenway. Dir. John Brett. <u>Sixty Minutes</u>. CBS
    WCBS, New York. 6 Mar. 1994.

SOUND RECORDING

Cite first whichever is emphasized: composer, performer, conductor, then title, artists, audiocassette, or LP if not a CD, manufacturer, date or N.D. if unknown.

Webber, Andrew Lloyd. <u>Phantom of the Opera</u>. Perf.
    Michael Crawford, Sarah Brightman, and Steve
    Barton. Audiocassette. EMI, 1987.

MLA WORKS CITED SAMPLES

FILM

Include title, director. Also if pertinent, writers, performers, producers, distributor, year.

Raiders of the Lost Ark. Dir. Steven Spielberg.
    Paramount, 1982.

INTERVIEW—BROADCAST

Gramm, Phil. Interview with Charlie Rose. Charlie
    Rose. WNET, New York. 6 May 1994.

INTERVIEW—PERSONAL

Kennedy, Robert. Personal Interview. 11 Jan. 1971.

CD-ROM—DISKETTE—MAGNETIC TAPE

Include author, title, date, database, CD-ROM or diskette or magnetic tape, vendor, electronic publication date

CD-ROM—PERIODICAL

United States. Dept. of Commerce. "Railroad Tonnage
    Reports." 1993. National Trade Data Bank. CD-ROM.
    US Dept. of Commerce. Apr. 1994.

CD-ROM—PERIODICAL ALSO PUBLISHED IN PRINT

Barron, James. "New York Welfare Programs in
    Jeopardy." New York Times 8 May 1995, late ed.:
    C1. New York Times Ondisc. CD-ROM. UMI-Proquest.
    Nov. 1995.

DISKETTE

Bernstein, Harold J. A History of Crime in America.
    Diskette. Columbus: U of Ohio P, 1994.

MAGNETIC TAPE

English Poetry Full-Text Database. Rel. 2. Magnetic
    Tape. Cambridge, Eng.: Chadwyck, 1993.

COMPUTER SERVICES

BRS—Dow Jones News Retrieval—Dialog—Prodigy—OCLC—Compuserve—Nexis—New York Times Online—America Online—Etc.

Include author, title, date, database title, online, computer service, access date.

Rich, Frank. "End of an Era in the Middle East." New
    York Times 8 May 1995, late ed.: C1. New York
    Times Online. Online. Nexis. 15 June 1995.

COMPUTER SERVICES

Studies of Pre-Kindergarten Programs 1983-93. Urbana:
   ERIC Clearinghouse on Elementary and Early Childhood Educ., 1994. ERIC. Online. BRS. 28 Oct. 1994.

DATABASE PUBLISHED WITH NO PRINT SOURCE SPECIFIED

"Civil War." Academic American Encyclopedia. Online.
   Prodigy. 15 Apr. 1994.

ELECTRONIC JOURNALS—NEWSLETTERS— CONFERENCES—INTERNET

Include author, title, newsletter or journal or conference title, volume or
issue, date, number of pages, or *n. pag.* if not paginated, online, computer
network, access date, electronic address preceded with word *available* if
required.

ELECTRONIC JOURNAL

Rabine, Richard. "Perseveration in Driving Habits."
   Psychologuy (June 1993): 9 pp. Online. Internet.
   11 Nov. 1994.

Lovett, Richard. "Teacher Traits." Psychologuy (June
   1994): 5 pp. Online. Internet. 6 Oct. 1993. Available FTP: Hostname:duke.eduDirectory:
   pub/harnad/Psychologuy/1993.

FILE TRANSFER PROTOCOL

Rabine, Richard. "Perseveration in Driving Habits."
   Psychologuy (June 1993) FTP: Hostname:duke.
   eduDirectory:pub/harnad/Psychologuy/1993.Volume.4.
   File:psycoloquy.93.4.13.base-rate.12.rabine.

E-MAIL

Lovett, Richard. "Discussion of Teacher Traits,"
   Psychololquy (June 1993) E-mail: psych@ducc
   Message: Get psyc 93-xxxx.

ELECTRONIC TEXT

Include author, title, print publication date, online, electronic text repository, computer network, access date, electronic address preceded with word
available if required.

Bronte, Emily. Collected Poems. Ed. Joseph Schmidt.
   London: Oxford UP, 1981. Online. U of California
   Lib. Internet. 12 Oct. 1995. Available: gopher
   ocf.berkeley.edu/OCF On-line Library/Poetry

SAMPLE *MLA* FIRST TEXT PAGE (TITLE PAGE)
WITH AUTHOR-PAGE CITATION

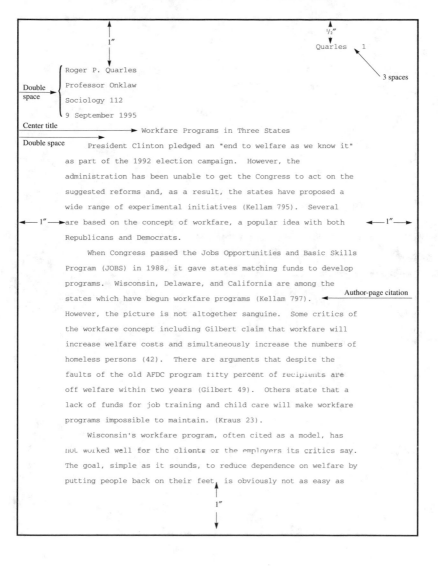

1″

½″

Quarles   1

3 spaces

Roger P. Quarles

Double space — Professor Onklaw

Sociology 112

9 September 1995

Center title — Workfare Programs in Three States

Double space

President Clinton pledged an "end to welfare as we know it" as part of the 1992 election campaign. However, the administration has been unable to get the Congress to act on the suggested reforms and, as a result, the states have proposed a wide range of experimental initiatives (Kellam 795). Several

1″ — are based on the concept of workfare, a popular idea with both   1″ Republicans and Democrats.

When Congress passed the Jobs Opportunities and Basic Skills Program (JOBS) in 1988, it gave states matching funds to develop programs. Wisconsin, Delaware, and California are among the states which have begun workfare programs (Kellam 797). — Author-page citation However, the picture is not altogether sanguine. Some critics of the workfare concept including Gilbert claim that workfare will increase welfare costs and simultaneously increase the numbers of homeless persons (42). There are arguments that despite the faults of the old AFDC program fifty percent of recipients are off welfare within two years (Gilbert 49). Others state that a lack of funds for job training and child care will make workfare programs impossible to maintain. (Kraus 23).

Wisconsin's workfare program, often cited as a model, has not worked well for the clients or the employers its critics say. The goal, simple as it sounds, to reduce dependence on welfare by putting people back on their feet, is obviously not as easy as

1″

AUTHOR-PAGE CITATION

SAMPLE *MLA* TEXT PAGE
WITH AUTHOR-PAGE CITATION

1"

it seems.   Still there are some successes and the lessons learned from the experimentation of the states has been invaluable.   The problem is a major one for America as seen by the statistics. Ten years ago fewer than four million families received welfare. Currently, five million families with about 14 million people receive benefits under the welfare system (Kellam 499).

Delaware's Department of Health and Social Services implemented its First Step Employment and Training Program in 1986, even before Federal legislation under the JOBS program. Under the current system, applicants eligible for Aid to Families with Dependent Children must enroll in an educational program, which frequently leads to a general equivalency diploma (GED). Candidates may be referred to the Delaware Technical and Community College for eight weeks of training in "life skills." With intitiative, some qualify for degrees from the college with support from regular monthly benefit payments, child care and Medicaid (Kaus 23).

1" ←→

1" ←→

Author-page citation

About 1.1 billion dollars in federal aid was available under the JOBS program to states capable of putting up matching funds. The federal government provided 1.8 million dollars to Delaware and the state matched with $978,558.   The state now operates 12 multi-service centers that serve as one stop facilities for individuals and families seeking federal aid (Kellam 796).

As late as August, 1995 President Clinton and Senator Dole presented different visions of welfare reform to state governors. Clinton took administrative action to approve state programs which put welfare recipients to work and which denied increases in food stamps to those who will not take jobs (Mitchell 1).

1"

SAMPLE *MLA* WORKS CITED PAGE

Works Cited

Bernstein, Phillip R., Charles D. Delanson, and Paul Connelson.
    "Attitudinal Changes in Mothers Engaged in Job Training."
    Journal of Applied Psychology 78 (1993): 452-457.

Carlson, Roberta J. The Dream and the Dilemma: Welfare in
    America. New York: Macmillan, 1994.

Conniff, Ruth. "Cutting the Lifeline: The Real Welfare Fraud."
    The Progressive Feb. 1992: 25-28

Cowan, Noah. "The Big Lie About Workfare." Utne Reader May-
    June 1992: 28-29.

Gilbert, Neil. "Why the New Workfare Won't Work." Commentary
    May 1994: 47.

Kaus, Mickey. "Tough Enough: A Promising Start on Welfare
    Reform." The New Republic 25 Apr. 1994: 22-23.

Kellam, Susan. "Welfare Experiments: Are States Leading the Way
    Toward National Reform?" Congressional Quarterly Researcher
    16 Sept.1994: 795-796.

Robinson, Karl, and Bernard R. Politcheck. The Politics of
    Welfare Reform. New York: McGraw Hill, 1994.

Schwartz, Miriam. "The Role of the Mother in AFDC Families."
    Consulting Psychology Journal: Practice and Research 45.4
    (1993): 27-29.

United States. Dept. of Health and Human Services. Survey of
    Jobs Training Programs. Washington: GPO, 1992.

"Workfare Debate Heats Up in Legislatures." Washington Post 21
    Aug. 1993: A3.

Word Processing the Paper

Locate the instructions for your word processor in this section by using the tabs on the side margins. Complete instructions and computer keystrokes for page layouts and special formats required by the *MLA Handbook for Writers of Research Papers* are shown.

Author-Page Citation with WordPerfect 4.2–5.1–6.0 for DOS

MARGINS

The setting for *MLA* papers is one inch on top, bottom and sides. This is the WordPerfect default setting. You need to adjust top margin to one half inch to properly place the page number header. Do not right justify or hyphenate.

WordPerfect 6.0.

1. Move the cursor to the top of the first page.
2. Press Shift+F8. The Format menu appears.
3. Press M for Margins, T for Top and type .5".
4. Press F7 three times.

WordPerfect 4.2–5.1

1. Move the cursor to the top of the first page.
2. Press Shift+F8. The Format menu appears.
3. Press P for Page and M for Margins. The cursor will move to Top.
4. Type .5".
5. Press F7, F7.

LINE SPACING

MLA papers are double spaced throughout.

1. Move the cursor to the top of the first page.
2. Press Shift+F8, L for Line and S for Spacing.
3. Press 2 for double spacing.
4. Press F7 twice in 4.2–5.1 and three times in 6.0.

PAGINATION

MLA papers carry a right justified heading one half inch from the top with your last name in upper and lower case and the page number in Arabic numerals beginning with the first page.

WordPerfect 6.0

1. Move the cursor to the top of the first page.
2. Press Shift+F8 and H. The Header/Footer/Watermark dialog box appears.
3. Press H and Enter, Enter to select Header A and All Pages.
4. Type your last name in upper and lower case and leave three spaces.
5. Press Shift+F8, P, N, and I to insert page numbers. The number 1 appears.
6. Move cursor to the left margin just before the first letter of your name.
7. Press Alt+F6 to move header to right margin.
8. Press Shift+F7 and V for View to see the header in preview.
9. Press F7, F7 to return to your paper.

WordPerfect 4.2–5.1

1. Move the cursor to the top of the first page.
2. Press Shift+F8, P for Page, H for Header,and A.
3. Press 2 for Every Page.
4. Type your last name in upper and lower case and leave three spaces.
5. Press Ctrl+B to insert page numbers. The number 1 appears.
6. Move cursor to the left margin just before the first letter of your name and press F7, F7.
7. Press Alt+F6 to move header to right margin.

8. Press Shift+F7 and V for View to check position of the header in preview.

9. Press F7, F7 to return to your paper.

INDENTION

MLA papers are indented five spaces. The WordPerfect default setting is one half inch. The correct tab setting depends on the font used.

1. Move the cursor to the top of the first page.

2. Press Shift+F8, L and T for Tab Set. The Tab ruler appears.

3. Count five characters from the left margin to locate the new first tab position in inches on the ruler.

4. Press the left or right arrow keys to position the new first tab stop and press L to set the new first tab.

5. Move the cursor to the old first tab stop and press Delete.

6. Press F7 three times to return to your text.

TITLE PAGE

1. Move the cursor to the top line of the first page.

2. Type in upper and lower case, your full name, first name first, on the top line, the instructor's name on the second line, the course number on the third line and date on the fourth line, all double spaced at the left margin.

3. Double space and center the title in upper and lower case.

4. Double space and begin your paper.

AUTHOR-PAGE CITATIONS

Citations are placed directly in the text. No special keystrokes are necessary. Follow the samples on pages 29–32.

WORKS CITED PAGE

1. Press Ctrl+Enter to start a new page.

2. Center the words, Works Cited, in upper and lower case.

3. Press Enter and type entries in alpabetical order using the appropriate formats shown on pages 34–38 for the type of reference you are citing.

4. The first line of each entry begins at left margin with the following lines double spaced and indented five spaces. Double space between entries.

TABLES

WordPerfect 6.0

1. Move the cursor to the place in the text where the table will be inserted and double space.

2. Type Table 1 flush left in upper and lower case without a period.

3. Double space and type the title flush left in upper and lower case. Extra lines are centered and double spaced.

4. Press Alt+F7. The Columns/Table dialog box appears.

5. Press T for Tables and C for Create. The Create Table dialog box appears.

6. Type in number of columns. Arrow down, and type in number of rows and press Enter, Enter. The table appears.

7. Press F7, F7 to return to your text.

8. Type headers at the top of each column and enter data in each cell using tab and arrow keys. Center data and header titles in each cell.

9. Press Alt+F7, T, E for Edit, and Enter.

10. Press Ctrl+arrows to reduce width of each cell to slightly larger than the header.

11. Press 4 for Table and P for Position. Arrow down to Center and Press Enter.

12. Press F7. Table will be centered on your text page.

13. Adjust title so it is flush with the upper left margin of the table. Double space and resume typing text.

WordPerfect 4.2–5.1

1. Move the cursor to the place in the text where the table will be inserted.

2. Type Table 1 flush left in upper and lower case without a period.

3. Double space and type the title flush left in upper and lower case. Extra lines of titles are double spaced. Double space after title.

4. Press Alt+F7, T for Tables and C for Create. The Number of Columns prompt appears.

5. Type the number of columns (vertical) you need and press Enter. The Number of Rows prompt appears. Type the number of rows (horizontal) you need and press Enter. The table appears.

6. Press F7 to return to your text and type the header titles in the first row of the table. Enter data in each cell using Tab and arrow keys. Center the data and header titles in each box.

7. Press Alt+F7 to edit the table. Use Ctrl+arrow keys to reduce the width of each cell to slightly larger than the header.

8. Press O for Options, P for Position and C for Center, F7, F7. The entire table will be centerd on the page.

9. Center the title over the table.

10. Press Shift+F7 and V to view document and check table setup.

11. Press F7 to return to your text, double space and resume typing.

Author-Page Citation with Microsoft Word for DOS 5.0–6.0

MARGINS

The setting for *MLA* papers is one inch top, bottom and sides. The default setting for Microsoft Word is 1.25″ left and right and 1.00″ top and bottom. You need to adjust the left and right margins. Do not right justify or hyphenate.

Microsoft Word 6.0

1. Choose Margins from the Format Menu. The Section Margins dialog box appears.
2. Press L for Left and type 1″.
3. Press R for Right and type 1″.
4. Press U for Use as default and choose OK.

Microsoft Word 5.0

1. Press Esc, F for Format and D for Division.
2. Press M for Margins and Tab to move the highlight to the word, Left, and type 1″.
3. Press Tab to move the highlight to the word, Right, and type 1″.
4. Press Enter and Esc.
5. Press F, D, and L for Layout and Tab to division break.
6. Press spacebar to Continuous and press Enter.

LINE SPACING

MLA papers are double spaced throughout.

Microsoft Word 6.0

1. Select the entire document by pressing Shift+F10.
2. Press Ctrl+2

Microsoft Word 5.0

1. Select the entire document by pressing Shift+F10.
2. Press Esc, F and P for Paragraph.
3. Press tab to line spacing: 1 li.
4. Type 2 li and Enter.

or

1. Press Alt+2

PAGINATION

MLA papers carry a right justified heading one half inch from the top with your last name in upper and lower case and the page number in Arabic numerals beginning with the first page.

Microsoft Word 6.0

1. Press Ctrl+Home to move the cursor to the top of the first page.
2. Type your last name in upper and lower case.
3. Press Enter. Select your name by pressing F8 and arrow keys. Press Esc to stop selecting.
4. Choose View Layout to turn off View Layout mode.
5. Choose Header/Footer from the Format menu. The Header/Footer dialog box appears.
6. Choose Header in the Format as box and First, Odd, and Even in the Print on box. Choose OK. A caret (^) will appear at the left of your name.
7. Leave three spaces and type the word, page. Highlight it and press F3
8. Use the tab key to move the header to the right margin.
9. Place the cursor in the header.
10. Choose Page Numbers from the Insert menu. The Page Numbers dialog box appears. Leave the Page Number Position setting at None.
11. Choose the Arabic numbers and Choose OK.

Microsoft Word 5.0

1. Move the cursor to the first line of the document.
2. Type your last name in upper and lower case at the left margin. Leave three spaces and type the word, page.

3. Move the cursor to the first letter in page and press F8 to select the word, page.

4. Press F3. Parentheses appears around the word, page.

5. Press Home and F10 to select the entire header.

6. Press Esc, F for Format, R for Running Head. The word, Top, should be highlighted. The word, Yes, should be in parentheses for even and odd pages, and the word, Yes, should be in parentheses for the first page. If not, press Tab and spacebar to change the settings.

7. Press Enter. A (t) for top and a caret (^) appears at the left of your name.

8. Press Esc, F, and P for Paragraph. Press spacebar until alignment right is highlighted.

9. Press Enter.

INDENTION

MLA papers are indented five spaces. The Microsoft Word default setting is one half inch. The correct tab setting will depend on the font used.

Microsoft Word 6.0

1. Press Shift+F10 to select whole document.

2. Choose Paragraph from the the Format Menu. The Paragraph dialog box appears.

3. Type new setting in tenths; e.g., 0.6 or 0.7 and choose OK.

4. Type ten test characters without a space and press Tab. Count the number of characters in the new tab set. Adjust as needed.

Microsoft Word 5.0

1. Press Esc, F, and Tab. The highlight appears on the word, Set.

2. Press Enter. (Left) will be in parenthesis with prompt, FORMAT TAB SET position.

3. Type new setting in tenths; e.g., .6, or .7, and press Enter.

4. Type ten test characters without a space and press Tab.

5. Count the number of characters in the new tab set.

6. Adjust as needed.

TITLE PAGE

1. Move the cursor to the top of the first page.

2. Type in upper and lower case, your full name, first name first, on the top line, the instructor's name on the second line, the course number on the third line and date on the fourth line, double spaced at the left margin.

3. Double space and center the title in upper and lower case. Double space and begin your paper.

AUTHOR-PAGE CITATIONS

Citations are placed directly in the text. No special keystrokes are necessary. Follow the samples on pages 29–32.

WORKS CITED PAGE

1. Press Ctrl, Shift, Enter to start a new page. Center the words, Works Cited, in upper and lower case.

2. Press Enter and type entries in alphabetical order using the appropriate formats shown on pages 34–38 for the type of reference you are citing.

3. The first line of each entry begins at left margin with the following lines double spaced and indented five spaces. Double space between entries.

TABLES

Microsoft Word 6.0

1. Move the cursor to the place in the text where the table will be inserted and double space.

2. Type Table 1 flush left without a period.

3. Double space and type the title flush left in upper and lower case. Extra lines are of title are centered and double spaced.

4. Choose Insert Table from the Table menu. The Insert Table dialog box appears.

5. Type in the number of columns (vertical) you need.

6. Type in the number of rows (horizontal) you need.

7. Press B to place lines around cells.

8. Choose OK and the table grid appears in your text.

9. Type headers at the top of each column and enter data in each cell using tab and arrow keys.

10. Center data and header titles in each cell using regular formatting.

11. Select Column Width from the Table menu. The dialog box appears.

12. Type the width in inches for each column as needed. Choose OK.

13. Center the table by selecting it and pressing Ctrl+C.

14. Double space and resume typing.

Microsoft Word 5.0

1. Move the cursor to the place in the text where the table will be inserted and double space.

2. Type Table 1 flush left without a period.

3. Double space and type the title flush left in upper and lower case. Extra lines of title are centered and double spaced.

4. Press O for Options, arrow to Yes for show ruler and Enter.

5. Press Esc, F, T for Tab, S for Set, and F1. A cursor appears on the ruler. Use arrow keys to move tabs to the locations for the columns.

6. Count the letters in the first header. If the first header title is the word, Subjects, the tab should be four spaces to the right of the T in Table.

7. Press C for Center alignment so data will be centered in the column.

8. Continue using arrow keys and pressing C at each stop estimating the space needed for each column and press Enter.

9. Type the headers. Press Shift+Enter twice at the end of each row. A small vertical arrow appears. This will start a new line, but keep the data in the same paragraph.

10. Enter the data using tabs. If you need to adjust the columns, highlight the table under the title.

11. Press Esc, F, T, S, and F1. Press Up or Down arrows to move to the tab you want to change.

12. Press Ctrl+Left or Right arrow to move tab stop and press Enter. Repeat for other stops.

13. Insert horizontal rules by pressing hyphen key.

Author-Page Citation with
WordPerfect for Windows 5.2–6.0

MARGINS

The setting for *MLA* papers is one inch on top, bottom and sides. This is the Wordperfect default setting. You need to adjust the top margin to one half inch to properly place the page number header. Do not right justify or hyphenate.

1. Click on Layout and Margins in the Menu Bar. The Margins dialog box appears. The Left box will be flashing.
2. Click on Top, press Delete and type in .5".
3. Click on OK.

LINE SPACING

MLA papers are double spaced throughout.

1. Click on Layout, Line and Spacing in the Menu Bar. The Line Spacing dialog box appears. The default setting is 1.
2. Click twice on the up arrow to change the setting to 2.
3. Click on OK.

or

1. Click on View and Ruler in the Button Bar. The Ruler appears.
2. Click on the last button on the right of the Button Bar.
3. Drag down to 2.0 lines and release.

PAGINATION

MLA papers carry a right justified heading one half inch from the top with your last name in upper and lower case and the page number in Arabic numerals beginning with the first page.

1. Move the cursor to the top of the first page and click on View and Ruler in the Menu Bar.
2. Click Layout, Page and Headers in the Menu Bar. The Headers dialog box appears with Header A selected.

WORDPERFECT WINDOWS

3. Click on Create. The Header window appears with the cursor at the left margin.

4. Type your last name in upper and lower case.

5. Click on Placement. The Placement dialog box appears with Every Page selected.

6. Click on OK. Move the cursor three spaces to the right of your name.

7. Click on Page Number. A ^B symbol appears.

8. Move the cursor to the first letter of your name. Click on the Justification button in the ruler and drag down to Right. The header will move to the right margin.

9. Click on Close. The cursor will return to your text.

INDENTION

MLA papers are indented five spaces. The Wordperfect for Windows default setting is one half inch. The correct tab setting depends on the font used.

1. Type an unbroken line of 15 characters.

2. Press Tab and count the number of spaces at the default tab setting. If correct, leave the setting. If not:

3. Click on Layout, Line, and Tab Set in the Menu Bar. The Tab Set dialog box appears with default setting in the Relative Position box.

4. Click on Clear Tabs.

5. Try typing 0.4 in the Relative Position Box.

6. Click on Tab Set and OK. The tab will be set for .4".

7. Press Tab and check the number of spaces at the new tab setting. Adjust as needed.

TITLE PAGE

1. Move the cursor to the top line of the first page.

2. Type in upper and lower case, your full name, first name first, on the top line, the instructor's name on the second line, the course number on the third line, and date on the fourth line all double spaced at the left margin.

3. Double space and center the title in upper and lower case.

4. Double space and begin your paper.

AUTHOR-PAGE CITATION

Citations are placed directly in the text. No special keystrokes are necessary. Follow the samples on pages 29–32.

WORDPERFECT WINDOWS

WORKS CITED PAGE

1. Press Ctrl+Enter to start a new page.
2. Center the words, Works Cited, in upper and lower case.
3. Press Enter and type entries in alphabetical order using the appropriate formats shown on pages 34–38 for the type of reference you are citing.
4. The first line of each entry begins at left margin with the following lines double spaced and indented five spaces. Double space between entries.

TABLES

WordPerfect for Windows 5.2–6.0

1. Move the cursor to the place in the text where the table will be inserted. Double space.
2. Type Table 1 flush left in upper and lower case without a period.
3. Double space and type the title flush left in upper and lower case. Extra lines are centered and double spaced. Double space.
4. Click on View and Ruler in the Menu Bar. The Ruler appears.
5. Click on the Table button in the ruler and drag down to the number of columns (vertical) and rows (horizontal) you want and release. The table appears spread across the screen.
6. Move the cursor from cell to cell with the arrow keys.
7. Enter the headers and data in each cell.
8. To adjust width of cells, drag the triangular markers above the ruler which separate the columns.
9. To center headers or data, select cells and click on the Justification button in the ruler. Drag down to Center and release.
10. To align decimal points, select the cells with decimal data, click on the Justification button in the ruler. Pull down to Decimal and release.
11. Move the entire table by clicking on Layout, Tables and Options. Click on Center in the Position box and click OK.
12. Select the entire table. Click on Layout, Tables and Lines. Select line styles as appropriate.
13. Click on File and Preview to check table setup.

Author-Page Citation with
Microsoft Word for Windows 2.0–6.0

MARGINS

The setting for *MLA* papers is one inch on top, bottom and sides. The default setting for Microsoft Word for Windows is 1.25″ left and right and 1″ top and bottom. You need to adjust the left and right margins. Do not right justify or hyphenate.

1. Click on Format and Page Setup in the Menu Bar. The Page Setup dialog box appears.
2. Click on Margins on the top line. Move the cursor to the Left and Right boxes with the mouse.
3. Click on the down arrows in the boxes until 1" appears.
4. Choose Whole Document or This Point Forward, whichever is appropriate, in the Apply to list.
5. Click on OK.

LINE SPACING

MLA papers are double spaced throughout.

1. Place the cursor at the beginning of the document.
2. Press Ctrl+2.

PAGINATION

MLA papers carry a right justified heading one half inch from the top with your last name in upper and lower case and the page number in Arabic numerals beginning with the first page.

Microsoft Word for Windows 6.0

1. Move the cursor to the top of the first page.
2. Click on View and Header/Footer in the Menu Bar. A Header/Footer toolbar appears in the center of the screen with a dotted box marked Header. The cursor will be inside the box at the left margin.

3. Type your last name in upper and lower case. Leave three spaces.

4. Click on the Page Number button with the # sign on the Header tool-bar.. The number 1 appears three spaces after your name.

5. Press Ctrl+R to align the header with the right margin.

6. Press Close.

Microsoft Word for Windows 2.0

1. Move the cursor to the top of the first page.

2. Click on View in the Menu Bar and be sure you are in Normal View.

3. Click on View and Header/Footer from the Menu Bar. The Header/Footer dialog box appears. Choose Header and OK. A Header window appears with the cursor at the left margin.

4. Type your last name in upper and lower case. Leave three spaces.

5. Click on the Page Number button with the # sign on the Header tool-bar. The number 1 appears three spaces after your name.

6. Press Ctrl+R to align header with the right margin.

7. Click on Close.

INDENTION

MLA papers are indented five spaces. The Word for Windows default set-ting is one half inch. The correct tab setting will depend on the font used.

Microsoft Word For Windows 6.0

1. Click on View and Ruler in the Menu Bar. The ruler appears.

2. Click on the box at the left end of the ruler until the symbol L appears.

3. Type an unbroken series of at least 15 characters at the left margin.

4. Click inside the ruler where the fifth character is located and release. The new first tab is set.

Microsoft Word For Windows 2.0

1. Click on View and Ruler in the Menu Bar. The ruler appears.

2. Type an unbroken series of at least 15 characters at the left margin.

3. Count 5 characters from the left margin.

4. Click on the tab marker at the .5″ mark on the ruler and drag it to the fifth character location and release. The new first tab is set.

TITLE PAGE

1. Move the cursor to the top line of the first page.

2. Type in upper and lower case, your full name, first name first, on the top line, the instructor's name on the second line, the course number on the third line and date on the fourth line, double spaced at the left margin.

3. Double space and center the title in upper and lower case. Double space and begin your paper.

AUTHOR-PAGE CITATIONS

Citations are placed directly in the text. No special keystrokes are necessary. Follow the examples on pages 29–32.

WORKS CITED PAGE

1. Click on Insert and Break in the Menu Bar to start a new page. The Break dialog box appears with Page Break selected.

2. Center the words, Works Cited, in upper and lower case on the top line. Double space.

3. Type entries in alphabetical order using the appropriate format shown on pages 34–38 for the type of reference you are citing. First line of each entry begins at left margin with following lines double spaced and indented five spaces.

4. Double space between entries.

TABLES

Microsoft Word for Windows 2.0 and 6.0

1. Move the cursor to the place in the text where the table will be inserted. Leave three blank lines.

2. Type Table 1 flush left without a period.

3. Double space and type the title flush left in upper and lower case. Extra lines of title are centered and double spaced.

4. Click on the Insert Table button just above the B, *I*, U buttons in the upper toolbar. A table box appears.

5. Drag across the columns (vertical) and rows (horizontal) until you have the correct number of cells you need.

6. Move the cursor from cell to cell with the tab or arrow keys. Do not use Enter in the table.

MICROSOFT WORD WINDOWS

7. Enter headers and data in each cell.

8. Click on Table in the Menu Bar and Select Table.

9. Click on Center button in the standard toolbar and all data in each cell will be centered.

10. Adjust the outside lines of the table by clicking on them. The cursor becomes two vertical lines with arrows pointing left and right. Drag the lines to the left and right edges of the table title.

11. Adjust the width of the columns by clicking on vertical lines and dragging them where you want them.

12. Move the cursor into the table and click on Table and the Center button in the toolbar.

4 Author-Date Citation

Publication Manual of the American Psychological Association, **4th Ed., 1994**

PARENTHETICAL AUTHOR-DATE CITATION TECHNIQUE

This is an easy way to cite sources. The author's last name and the date of publication of the work where the material can be found are placed in parentheses in the text. A little practice may be necessary to insert the references and keep the writing fluent. Samples of common parenthetical references are below.

A bibliography, called References, printed on a separate page at the end of the paper, provides complete publication information.

WORK—SINGLE AUTHOR

Insert last name of author and year of publication in parentheses in the text.

```
A study of reactive inhibition (Rogers,
1979)...
```

or

If author's name appears in text, insert only the year of the work in parentheses.

```
Roger's (1979) study of reactive inhibition
indicated...
```

Second or later mention of same work. The year within parentheses may be omitted if there will be no confusion.

```
In his study of reactive inhibition, Rogers
also found...
```

PARENTHETICAL AUTHOR-DATE
CITATION TECHNIQUE

WORK—TWO AUTHORS
Mention of a work by two authors should always include both names separated by an *ampersand (&)* in the parentheses or the word *and* in the text.

In an explanation of mental disorder, (Rogers & Phillips, 1978) described...

Rogers and Phillips (1978) studied mental disorder...

WORK—MULTIPLE AUTHORS
First mention of a work by three or more authors should include all the authors.

Published studies which illustrate the P technique (Cattel, Smith & Rhymer, 1947) stress the relationship...

Later mention of a work by three or more authors may be shortened to last name of first author and the Latin abbreviation, et al., (no period after et) and the year only if there is no confusion.

In a study of P technique, Cattel et al. (1947) stress...

Include initials of authors with the same name

CORPORATE AUTHOR
On first mention name should be spelled out in text.

Statistical reports on homosexuality in the armed forces (National Institute of Mental Health [NIMH], 1989) indicated...

Subsequent mention may be abbreviated if not confusing.

The study of homosexuality (NIMH, 1989) indicated...

WORK—NO NAMED AUTHOR
Use short title and date for the parenthetical citation

Latest study of the brain reveals new understandings of brain waves ("New Brain Study," 1995).

QUOTATIONS

Quotations of 40 words or fewer are not set off from the text but are placed within double quotation marks. Use single quotation marks for quotation within a short quotation.

For longer quotations, use colon after the last word of text, double space, indent five spaces and type in a block without paragraph indentation. Do not use quotation marks. Double space quotation. If more than one paragraph, indent paragraphs five spaces from new margin. Use double quotation marks for a quotation within a long quotation.

REFERENCES—BIBLIOGRAPHY

The bibliography is called References in APA style. The short parenthetical references in your text lead the reader to the list of sources found on the page following the last line of your paper. Entries are alphabetized letter by letter by author's last names, association or title if author is not known. Entries are shown single-spaced to conserve space in this book, **but they must be double-spaced in your paper.**

APA REFERENCE SAMPLES

BOOKS

BOOK—NO AUTHOR

Psychology and you (1990). New York: Macmillan.

BOOK—ONE AUTHOR

Helmstadter, G. C. (1991). Research concepts in human behavior. New York: Houghton.

BOOK—MULTIPLE AUTHORS

Mathews, T. R., & Lawser, P. Q. (1993). Theories of management. New York: McGraw-Hill.

BOOK—CORPORATE AUTHOR

American Psychological Association. (1994). Publication manual of the American Psychological Association (4th ed.). Washington, DC: American Psychological Association.

BOOK—MULTIVOLUME

Brosnia, R. (Ed.). (1989). Personality: Theory and practice (Vols. 1–4). New York: Macmillan.

BOOK—EDITOR INSTEAD OF AUTHOR

Feigenbaum, E., & Feldman, J. (Eds.). (1991). Computers and thought. New York: McGraw-Hill.

BOOK—REVISED EDITION

Robertson, J. (1989). Contemporary issues in psychology (Rev. ed.). New York: Praeger.

ARTICLE OR CHAPTER IN EDITED BOOK

Schwartz, R. P. (1990). Learning styles. In F.S. Keenan & L.F. Bird (Eds.), Education for the nineties (pp. 312–322). New York: Avon.

DIAGNOSTIC AND STATISTICAL MANUAL OF MENTAL DISORDERS

American Psychiatric Association. (1994). Diagnostic and statistical manual of mental disorders (4th ed.). Washington, DC: Author.

ENCYCLOPEDIA ARTICLE—SIGNED

Johnson, R. S. (1994). Radioactivity. In The new encyclopedia Britannica (Vol. 25, pp. 453–455). Chicago: Encyclopedia Britannica.

PERIODICALS

JOURNAL ARTICLE—ONE AUTHOR

Braverman, D. (1962). Normative and ipsative measurement in psychology. <u>Psychological Review, 69,</u> 295-305.

JOURNAL PAGINATED BY ISSUE AND NUMBER—
ARTICLE—TWO AUTHORS

Roberts, J. R., & Smithson, B. (1975). Family orientations of Chinese college students. <u>Journal of Marriage and the Family, 34</u>(4), 29-37.

JOURNAL ARTICLE—THREE TO FIVE AUTHORS

Bronkowski, L. P., Johnson, R. J., Oppenheimer, K. S., & Pushkin, B. J. (1994). Age as a factor in flight performance. <u>Journal of Applied Psychology, 79,</u> 421-427.

MAGAZINE ARTICLE

Horowitz, C. H. (1994, October 10). Is Rikers about to explode? <u>New York, 27,</u> 29-37.

NEWSPAPER ARTICLE—SIGNED

Barron, J. (1995, June 30). Brain studies give clues on depression. <u>New York Times,</u> pp. A1, A3.

MONOGRAPH WITH ISSUE NUMBER
AND SERIAL OR WHOLE NUMBERS

Coswell, R., & Klingenstein, P. R. (1965). A computer model of personality. <u>Psychological Monographs, 79</u>(1, Whole No. 540).

MONOGRAPH BOUND SEPARATELY
AS JOURNAL SUPPLEMENT

Johnson, P. Q., & Pritchard, K. (1969). Creativity. <u>Journal of Experimental Psychology Monographs, 80,</u>(1, Pt. 2).

MONOGRAPH BOUND IN JOURNAL
WITH CONTINUOUS PAGES

Hirsch, J., & Brown, R. W. (1974). Analysis of bias in selecting test times [Monograph]. <u>Journal of Experimental Psychology, 98,</u> 325-331.

REPORTS

GOVERNMENT PRINTING OFFICE REPORT

United States Public Health Service. (1990). Statistical tables for medical research (USPHS Publication No. 37). Washington, DC: U.S. Government Printing Office.

REPORT DIRECT FROM GOVERNMENT AGENCY

U.S. Department of Health and Human Services. (1994). Breast cancer: geographic studies (AHCPR Publication No. 94-0313). Rockville, MD: Author.

NATIONAL TECHNICAL INFORMATION SERVICE (NTIS) REPORT

Braveson, R. B., & Rogers, E. S. (1992). Authentic assessment and teacher variables. Ann Arbor: University of Michigan. (NTIS No. RS 93-721 215/KR).

EDUCATIONAL RESOURCES INFORMATION CENTER (ERIC) REPORT

Cook, J. V. (1992). Teaching styles Report No. NCRTL-RJ-46-3). New York, NY: Center for Research on Teaching. (ERIC Document Reproduction Service No. ED 241 079)

DOCTORAL DISSERTATIONS

DOCTORAL DISSERTATION IN DISSERTATION ABSTRACTS INTERNATIONAL OBTAINED FROM A UNIVERSITY

Baron, A. (1990). The use of personality factors as criteria for grouping pupils for computer instruction (Doctoral dissertation, New York University, 1990). Dissertation Abstracts International, 49, 4379A.

DOCTORAL DISSERTATION IN DISSERTATION ABSTRACTS INTERNATIONAL OBTAINED ON UNIVERSITY MICROFILM

Baron, A. (1990). The use of personality factors as criteria for grouping pupils for computer instruction. Dissertation Abstracts International, 49, 4379A. (University Microfilms No. ABD72-13497)

UNPUBLISHED DOCTORAL DISSERTATION

Smeterna, C. K. (1993). Stuttering and its effects on academic achievement. Unpublished doctoral dissertation, University of Michigan, Ann Arbor.

REVIEWS

REVIEW OF BOOK, FILM OR VIDEO

Shanahan, P. M. (1994). Challenging the giants [Review of the book Freud and Jung]. Contemporary Psychology, 39, 321-322.

AUDIOVISUAL SOURCES

TELEVISION—EPISODE FROM A SERIES

Moyers, B. (1995). The field of time (D. Grubin, Producer-Director). In The language of life with Bill Moyers. New York: WNET.

SOUND RECORDING

Browning, R. Z. (Speaker). (1991). Treatment of phobia (Cassette Recording No. 419-212-79A-B). Washington, DC: American Psychological Association.

ELECTRONIC SOURCES

ON-LINE ABSTRACT AVAILABLE THROUGH COMPUTER SERVICE

Cunningham, W. J., & O'Reilly, L. (1991). Drug therapy and recidivism [On-line]. Journal of Applied Psychology, 76, 112-117. Abstract from: DIALOG File: PsycINFO Item: 79-13456

ON-LINE JOURNAL—FILE TRANSFER PROTOCOL

Rogers, R. R. (1993, June). Perserveration in driving habits [4 paragraphs]. Psycholoquy [On-line serial], 4(13). Available FTP: Hostname: duke.edu Directory:pub/harnad/Psycholoquy/1993.volume.4 File: psycoloquy.93.4.13.base-rate.12.rogers

E-MAIL

Rogers, R. R. (1993, June). Perseveration in driving habits [4 paragraphs]. Psycholoquy [On-line serial, 4(13). Available E-mail: psyc@ducc Message: Get psyc 93-xxxxx

ABSTRACT ON CD-ROM

King, A. J. (1992). Longitudinal study of stuttering [CD-ROM]. Journal of Applied Psychology, 77, 410-417. Abstract from: SilverPlatter File: PsycLIT Item: 79-18421.

SAMPLE *APA* TITLE PAGE

2–3 word brief title → Workfare Effectiveness   1

½″

←—1″—→ Running Head: EFFECTIVENESS OF WORKFARE IN THREE STATES

5 spaces

Abbreviated title—all caps
Not more than 50 characters
including punctuation and spaces

Center full title on page → Effectiveness of Workfare Programs in

Double space   Wisconsin, Delaware, and California from 1992 to 1994

Your name

Double space   Roger P. Quarles ←

Michigan State University ←

Your school

SAMPLE *APA* ABSTRACT PAGE

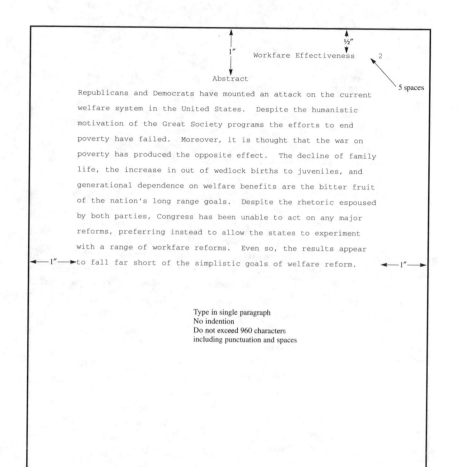

Workfare Effectiveness   2

Abstract

Republicans and Democrats have mounted an attack on the current welfare system in the United States. Despite the humanistic motivation of the Great Society programs the efforts to end poverty have failed. Moreover, it is thought that the war on poverty has produced the opposite effect. The decline of family life, the increase in out of wedlock births to juveniles, and generational dependence on welfare benefits are the bitter fruit of the nation's long range goals. Despite the rhetoric espoused by both parties, Congress has been unable to act on any major reforms, preferring instead to allow the states to experiment with a range of workfare reforms. Even so, the results appear to fall far short of the simplistic goals of welfare reform.

Type in single paragraph
No indention
Do not exceed 960 characters
including punctuation and spaces

AUTHOR-DATE CITATION

SAMPLE *APA* FIRST PAGE OF TEXT

Effectiveness of Workfare Programs in Wisconsin, Delaware, and California from 1992 to 1994

Full title centered

President Clinton pledged an "end to welfare as we know it" as part of the 1992 election campaign. However, the administration has been unable to get the Congress to act on the suggested reforms and, as a result, the states have proposed a wide range of experimental initiatives (Kellam, 1994). Several are based on the concept of workfare, a popular idea with both Republicans and Democrats.

When Congress passed the Jobs Opportunities and Basic Skills Program (JOBS) in 1988, it gave states matching funds to develop programs. Wisconsin, Delaware, and California are among the states which have begun workfare programs (Kellam, 1994). Author-date citation However, the picture is not altogether sanguine. Some critics of the workfare concept including Gilbert claim that workfare will increase welfare costs and simultaneously increase the numbers of homeless persons (1994). There are arguments that despite the faults of the old AFDC program fifty percent of recipients are off welfare within two years (Gilbert, 1994). Others state that a lack of funds for job training and child care will make workfare programs impossible to maintain. (Kraus, 1994).

Wisconsin's workfare program, often cited as a model, has not worked well for the clients or the employers say its critics (Conniff, 1992). The goal, simple as it sounds, to reduce dependence on welfare by putting people back on their feet, is obviously not as easy as it seems. Nevertheless, there have been

AUTHOR-DATE CITATION

SAMPLE *APA* REFERENCE PAGE

Double space

References

Bernstein, P. R., Delanson, C. D., & Connelson, P. (1993). Attitudinal changes in mothers engaged in job training. Journal of Applied Psychology, 78, 452-457.

Carlson, R. J. (1994). The dream and the dilemma: Welfare in America. New York: Macmillan.

Conniff, R. (1992, February). Cutting the lifeline: The real welfare fraud. The Progressive, 25-28.

Cowan, N. (1992, May-June). The big lie about workfare. Utne Reader, 28-29.

Gilbert, N. (1994, May) Why the new workfare won't work. Commentary, 47.

Kaus, M. (1994, April 25).s Tough enough: A promising start on welfare reform. The New Republic, 22-23.

Kellam, S. (1994, September 16). Welfare experiments: Are states leading the way toward national reform? Congressional Quarterly Researcher, 795-796.

Robinson, K., & Politcheck, B. R. (1994). The politics of welfare reform. New York: McGraw Hill

Schwartz, M. (1993). The role of the mother in AFDC families. Consulting Psychology Journal: Practice and Research, 45(4), 27-29.

U.S. Department of Health and Human Services. (1992). Survey of Jobs Training Programs (AHCPR Publication No. 92-0451). Rockville, MD: Author.

Workfare debate heats up in legislatures. (1993, August 21). The Washington Post, p. A3.

1"

½" indent

Word Processing the Paper

Locate the instructions for your word processor in this section by using the tabs on the side margins. Complete instructions and computer keystrokes for page layouts and special formats required by the *Publication Manual of the APA* are shown.

Author-Date Citation with
WordPerfect 4.2–5.1–6.0 for DOS

MARGINS

The setting for *APA* papers is one inch on top, bottom and sides. This is the WordPerfect default setting. You need to adjust top margin to one half inch to properly place the page number header. Do not right justify or hyphenate.

WordPerfect 6.0.

1. Move the cursor to the top of the first page.
2. Press Shift+F8. The Format menu appears.
3. Press M for Margins T for Top and type .5″.
4. Press F7 three times.

WordPerfect 4.2–5.1

1. Move the cursor to the top of the first page.
2. Press Shift+F8. The Format menu appears.
3. Press P for Page and M for Margins. The cursor will move to Top.
4. Type .5″.
5. Press F7, F7.

LINE SPACING

APA papers are double spaced throughout.

1. Move the cursor to the top of the first page.
2. Press Shift+F8, L for Line and S for Spacing.
3. Press 2 for double spacing.
4. Press F7 twice in **4.2–5.1** and three times in **6.0**.

PAGINATION

APA papers carry a right justified heading one half inch from the top with the first two or three words of the title in upper and lower case and the page number in Arabic numerals beginning with the first page.

WordPerfect 6.0

1. Move the cursor to the top of the first page.
2. Press Shift+F8 and H. The Header/Footer/Watermark dialog box appears.
3. Press H and Enter, Enter to select Header A and All Pages.
4. Type the first two or three words of the title in upper and lower case and leave five spaces.
5. Press Shift+F8, P, N, and I to insert page numbers. The number 1 appears.
6. Move cursor to the left margin just before the first letter of your name.
7. Press Alt+F6 to move header to right margin.
8. Press Shift+F7 and V for View to see the header in preview.
9. Press F7, F7 to return to your paper.

WordPerfect 4.2–5.1

1. Move the cursor to the top of the first page.
2. Press Shift+F8, P for Page, H for Header, and A.
3. Press 2 for Every Page.
4. Type the first two or three words of the title in upper and lower case and leave five spaces.
5. Press Ctrl+B to insert page numbers. The number 1 appears.
6. Move the cursor to the left margin just before the first letter of your name and press F7, F7.
7. Press Alt+F6 to move header to right margin.

8. Press Shift+F7 and V for View to see the header in preview.

9. Press F7, F7 to return to your paper.

INDENTION

APA papers are indented five to seven spaces. The WordPerfect default setting is one half inch. The correct tab setting depends on the font used.

1. Move the cursor to the top of the first page.

2. Press Shift+F8, L and T for Tab Set. The Tab ruler appears.

3. Count five to seven characters from the left margin to locate the new first tab position.

4. Press the left or right arrow keys to position the new first tab stop and press L to set the new first tab.

5. Move the cursor to the old first tab stop and press Delete.

6. Press F7 three times to return to your text.

TITLE PAGE

1. Move the cursor to the top line of the first page.

2. Type at the left margin the words, Running Head:, in upper and lower case, leave two spaces and type an abbreviated title of fewer than 50 characters in all upper case including punctuation and spaces.

3. Center the full title in upper and lower case on the page. Double space if two or more lines.

4. Center your name in upper and lower case one double space below the title.

5. Center your school name in upper and lower case one double space below your name.

ABSTRACT PAGE

1. Press Ctrl+Enter to begin page 2.

2. Center the word, Abstract, in upper and lower case on the top line and double space.

3. Type the abstract, a summary of your paper, in a single paragraph without paragraph indention in fewer than 960 characters including punctuation and spacing.

TEXT

1. Press Ctrl+Enter to begin page 3.

2. Center the title in upper and lower case double spaced at the top.

3. Double space and begin typing text. Do not start a new page when a new section begins.

AUTHOR-DATE CITATIONS

Citations are placed directly in the text. No special keystrokes are necessary. Follow the samples on pages 59–60.

REFERENCES PAGE

1. Press Ctrl+Enter to start a new page.

2. Center the word, References, in upper and lower case on the top line.

3. Press Enter and type the entries using the formats shown on pages 62–65 for the type of reference you are citing.

4. Double space within and between entries. Indent the first line five to seven spaces.

APPENDIXES

1. Press Ctrl+Enter to start a new page.

2. Center the word, Appendix, in upper and lower case on the top line.

3. Double space and center the title of the appendix in upper and lower case.

4. Double space and type the text double spaced with a regular paragraph indent.

TABLES

WordPerfect 6.0

1. Move the cursor to the place in the text where the table will be inserted. Double space.

2. Type Table 1 flush left in upper and lower case without a period.

3. Double space and type the title, flush left, underlined, in upper and lower case. Extra lines are double spaced flush left.

4. Press Alt+F7. The Columns/Table dialog box appears.

5. Press T for Tables and C for Create. The Create Table dialog box appears.

6. Type in number of columns. Arrow down, and type in number of rows and press Enter, Enter. The table appears.

7. Press F7, F7 to return to your text.

8. Type headers at the top of each column and enter data in each cell using tab and arrow keys. Center data in each cell.

9. Press Alt+F7, T, E for Edit, and Enter.

10. Press Ctrl+arrows to reduce width of each cell to slightly larger than the header.

11 Press 4 for Table and P for Position. Arrow down to Center and Press Enter.

12. Press F7. Table will be centered on your text page.

13. Adjust title so it is flush with the upper left margin of the table. Double space and and resume typing text.

WordPerfect 4.2–5.1

1. Move the cursor to the place in the text where the table will be inserted. Double space.

2. Type Table 1 flush left in upper and lower case without a period.

3. Double space and type the title flush left underlined in upper and lower case. Extra lines are double spaced flush left. Double space.

4. Press Alt+F7, T for Tables and C for Create. The Number of Columns prompt appears.

5. Type the number of columns (vertical) you need and press Enter. The Number of Rows prompt appears. Type the number of rows (horizontal) you need and press Enter. The table appears.

6. Press F7 to return to your text and type the header titles in the first row of the table. Enter data in each cell using Tab and arrow keys. Center the data and header titles in each box.

7. Press Alt+F7 to edit the table. Use Ctrl+arrow keys to reduce the width of each cell to slightly larger than the header.

8. Press O for Options, P for Position and C for Center, F7, F7. The entire table will be centered on the page.

9. Center the title over the table but second and third lines of titles are flush left with the table.

10. Press Shift+F7 and V to view document and check table setup.

11. Press F7 to return to your text, double space and resume typing.

Author-Date Citation with
Microsoft Word for DOS 5.0–6.0

MARGINS

The setting for *APA* papers is one inch top, bottom and sides. The default setting for Microsoft Word is 1.25" left and right and 1.00" top and bottom. Do not right justify or hyphenate.

Microsoft Word 6.0

1. Choose Margins from the Format Menu. The Section Margins dialog box appears.
2. Press L for Left and type 1".
3. Press R for Right and type 1".
4. Press U for Use as default and choose OK..

Microsoft Word 5.0

1. Press Esc, F for Format and D for Division.
2. Press M for Margins and Tab to move the highlight to the word, Left, and type 1".
3. Press Tab to move the highlight to the word, Right, and type in 1".
4. Press Enter.
5. Press Esc.
6. Press F, D, and L for Layout and Tab to division break.
7. Press spacebar to Continuous and Press Enter.

LINE SPACING

APA papers are double spaced throughout.

Microsoft Word 6.0

1. Select the entire document by pressing Shift+F10.
2. Press Ctrl+2

Microsoft Word 5.0

1. Select the entire document by pressing Shift+F10.
2. Press Esc, F and P for Paragraph.
3. Press tab to line spacing: 1 li.
4. Type 2 li and Enter.

or

1. Press Alt+2

PAGINATION

APA papers carry a right justified heading one half inch from the top with the first two or threee words of the title in upper and lower case and the page number in Arabic numerals beginning with the first page.

Microsoft 6.0

1. Press Ctrl+Home to move the cursor to the top of the first page.
2. Type the first two or three words of the title in upper and lower case.
3. Press Enter. Select the title by pressing F8 until it is highlighted. Press Esc to stop selecting.
4. Choose View Layout to turn off View Layout mode.
5. Choose Header/Footer from the Format menu. The Header/Footer dialog box appears.
6. Choose Header in the Format as box and First, Odd, and Even in the Print on box. Choose OK. A caret (^) will appear at the left of the title.
7. Leave five spaces and type the word, page. Highlight it and press F3.
8. Use the tab key to move the header to the right margin.
9. Place the cursor in the header.
10. Choose Page Numbers from the Insert menu. The Page Numbers dialog box appears. Leave the Page Number Position setting at None.
11. Choose Arabic numbers and choose OK.

Microsoft Word 5.0

1. Move the cursor to the first line of the document.
2. Type the first two or three words of the title in upper and lower case at the left margin. Leave five spaces and type the word, page. Move the cursor to the letter p in page and press F8 to select the word.

3. Press F3. Parentheses appears around the word, page.

4. Press Home and F10 to select the entire header.

5. Press Esc, F for Format, R for Running Head. The word, Top, should be highlighted. The word, Yes, should be in parentheses for even and odd pages, and the word, Yes, should be in parentheses for the first page. If not, press Tab and spacebar to change the settings.

6. Press Enter. A (t) for top and a caret (^) appears at the left of the short title.

7. Press Esc, F, and P for Paragraph. Press spacebar until alignment right is highlighted.

8. Press Enter.

INDENTION

APA papers are indented five to seven spaces. The Microsoft Word default setting is one half inch. The correct tab setting will depend on the font used.

Microsoft Word 6.0

1. Press Shift+F10 to select whole document.

2. Choose Paragraph from the the Format Menu. The Paragraph dialog box appears.

3. Type new setting in tenths; e.g., 0.6 or 0.7 and choose OK.

Microsoft Word 5.0

1. Press Esc, F, and Tab. The highlight appears on the word, Set.

2. Press Enter. (Left) will be in parenthesis with prompt, FORMAT TAB SET position:

3. Type new setting in tenths; e.g., .6, or .7, and press Enter.

TITLE PAGE

1. Move the cursor to the top line of the first page.

2. Type at the left margin the words, Running Head:, in upper and lower case, leave two spaces and type an abbreviated title of fewer than 50 characters in all upper case including punctuation and spaces.

3. Center the full title in upper and lower case on the page. Double space if more two or more lines.

4. Center your name in upper and lower case one double space below the title.

5. Center your school name in upper and lower case one double space below your name.

ABSTRACT PAGE

1. Press Ctrl+Shift+Enter to begin page 2.
2. Center the word, Abstract, in upper and lower case on the top line and double space.
3. Type the abstract, a summary of your paper, in a single paragraph without paragraph indention in fewer than 960 characters including punctuation and spacing.

TEXT

1. Press Ctrl+Shift+Enter to begin page 3.
2. Center the title in upper and lower case double spaced at the top.
3. Double space and begin typing text. Do not start a new page when a new section begins.

AUTHOR-PAGE CITATIONS

Citations are placed directly in the text. No special keystrokes are necessary. Follow the samples on pages 59–60.

REFERENCES PAGE

1. Press Ctrl+Shift+Enter to start a new page.
2. Center the word, References, in upper and lower case on the top line. Double space.
3. Type the entries using the formats shown on pages 62–65.
4. Double space within and between entries. Indent the first line five to seven spaces.

APPENDIXES

1. Press Ctrl+Shift+Enter to start a new page.
2. Center the word, Appendix, in upper and lower case on the top line.
3. Double space and center the title of the appendix in upper and lower case.
4. Double space and type the text double spaced with a regular paragraph indent.

TABLES

Microsoft Word 6.0

1. Move the cursor to the place in the text where the table will be inserted. Double space.
2. Type Table 1 flush left in upper and lower case without a period.
3. Double space and type the title flush left underlined in upper and lower case. Extra lines are double spaced flush left.
4. Choose Insert Table from the Table menu. The Insert Table dialog box appears.
5. Type in the number of columns (vertical) you need.
6. Type in the number of rows (horizontal) you need.
7. Press B to place lines around cells.
8. Choose OK and the table grid appears in your text.
9. Type headers at the top of each column and enter data in each cell using tab and arrow keys. Center data and header titles in each cell using regular formatting.
10. Select Column Width from the Table menu. The dialog box appears.
11. Type the width in inches for each column as needed.
12. Choose OK.
13. Center the table by selecting it and pressing Ctrl+C.
14. Double space and resume typing.

Microsoft Word 5.0

1. Move the cursor to the place in the text where the table will be inserted. Double space.
2. Type Table 1 flush left in upper and lower case without a period.
3. Double space and type the title flush left underlined in upper and lower case. Extra lines are double spaced flush left.
4. Press O for Options, arrow to Yes for show ruler and Enter.
5. Press Esc, F, T for Tab, S for Set, and F1. A cursor appears on the ruler. Use arrow keys to move tabs to the locations for the columns.
6. Count the letters in the first header. If the first header title is the word, Subjects, the tab should be four spaces to the right of the T in Table.
7. Press C for Center alignment so data will be centered in the column.

8. Continue using arrow keys and pressing C at each stop estimating the space needed for each column and press Enter.

9. Type the headers. Press Shift+Enter twice at the end of each row. A small vertical arrow appears. This will start a new line, but keep the data in the same paragraph.

10. Enter the data using tabs. If you need to adjust the columns, highlight the table under the title.

11. Press Esc, F, T, S, and F1. Press Up or Down arrows to move to the tab you want to change.

12. Press Ctrl+Left or Right arrow to move tab stop and press Enter. Repeat for other stops.

Author-Date Citation with
WordPerfect for Windows 5.2–6.0

MARGINS

The setting for *APA* papers is one inch on top, bottom and sides. This is the Wordperfect for Windows default setting. You need to adjust the top margin to one half inch to properly place the page number header. Do not right justify or hyphenate.

1. Click on Layout and Margins in the Menu Bar. The Margins dialog box appears. The Left box will be flashing.
2. Click on Top, press Delete and type in .5".
3. Click on OK.

LINE SPACING

APA papers are double spaced throughout.

1. Click on Layout, Line and Spacing in the Menu Bar. The Line Spacing dialog box appears. The default setting is 1.
2. Click twice on the up arrow to change the setting to 2.
3. Click on OK.

or

1. Click on View and Ruler in the Button Bar. The Ruler appears.
2. Click on the last button on the right of the Button Bar.
3. Drag down to 2.0 lines and release.

PAGINATION

APA papers carry a right justified heading one half inch from the top with the first two or three words of the title in upper and lower case and the page number in Arabic numerals beginning with the first page.

1. Move the cursor to the top of the first page and click on View and Ruler in the Menu Bar.
2. Click Layout, Page and Headers in the Menu Bar. The Headers dialog box appears with Header A selected.

3. Click on Create. The Header window appears with the cursor at the left margin.

4. Type the first two or three words of the title in upper and lower case.

5. Click on Placement. The Placement dialog box appears with Every Page selected.

6. Click on OK. Move the cursor five spaces to the right of the short title.

7. Click on Page Number. A ^B symbol appears.

8. Move the cursor to the first letter of the short title. Click on the Justification button in the ruler and drag down to Right. The header will move to the right margin.

9. Click on Close. The cursor will return to your text.

INDENTION

APA papers are indented five to seven spaces. The Wordperfect for Windows default setting is one half inch. The correct tab setting depends on the font used.

1. Type an unbroken line of 15 characters.

2. Press Tab and count the number of spaces at the default tab setting. If correct, leave the setting. If not:

3. Click on Layout, Line, and Tab Set in the Menu Bar. The Tab Set dialog box appears with default setting in the Relative Position box.

4. Click on Clear Tabs.

5. Try typing 0.7 in the Relative Position Box.

6. Click on Tab Set and OK. The tab will be set for .7".

7. Press Tab and check the number of spaces at the new tab setting. Adjust as needed.

TITLE PAGE

1. Move the cursor to the top line of the first page.

2. Type at the left margin the words, Running Head:, in upper and lower case, leave two spaces and type an abbreviated title of fewer than 50 characters in all upper case including punctuation and spaces.

3. Center the full title in upper and lower case on the page. Double space if more two or more lines.

4. Center your name in upper and lower case one double space below the title.

5. Center your school name in upper and lower case one double space below your name.

ABSTRACT PAGE

1. Press Ctrl+Enter to begin page 2.
2. Center the word, Abstract, in upper and lower case on the top line and double space.
3. Type the abstract, a summary of your paper, in a single paragraph without paragraph indention in fewer than 960 characters including punctuation and spacing.

TEXT

1. Press Ctrl+Enter to begin page 3.
2. Center the title in upper and lower case double spaced at the top.
3. Double space and begin typing text. Do not start a new page when a new section begins.

AUTHOR-DATE CITATION

Citations are placed directly in the text. No special keystrokes are necessary. Follow the samples on pages 59–60.

REFERENCES PAGE

1. Press Ctrl+Enter to start a new page.
2. Center the word, References, in upper and lower case on the top line. Double space.
3. Type the entries using the appropriate formats shown on pages 62–65 for the type of reference you are citing.
4. Double space within and between entries. Indent the first line five to seven spaces.

APPENDIXES

1. Press Ctrl+Enter to start a new page.
2. Center the word, Appendix, in upper and lower case on the top line.
3. Double space and center the title of the appendix in upper and lower case.
4. Double space and type the text double spaced with a regular paragraph indent.

WORDPERFECT WINDOWS

TABLES

WordPerfect for Windows 5.2–6.0

1. Move the cursor to the place in the text where the table will be inserted. Double space.

2. Type Table 1 flush left in upper and lower case without a period.

3. Double space and type the title flush left underlined in upper and lower case. Extra lines of titles are flush left. Double space.

4. Click on View and Ruler in the Menu Bar. The Ruler appears.

5. Click on the Table button in the ruler and drag down to the number of columns (vertical) and rows (horizontal) you want and release. The table appears spread across the screen.

6. Move the cursor from cell to cell with the arrow keys.

7. Enter the headers and data in each cell.

8. To adjust width of cells, drag the triangular markers above the ruler which separate the columns.

9. To center headers or data, select cells and click on the Justification button in the ruler. Drag down to Center and release.

10. To align decimal points, select the cells with decimal data, click on the Justification button in the ruler. Pull down to Decimal and release.

11. Move the entire table by clicking on Layout, Tables and Options. Click on Center in the Position box and click OK.

12. Select the entire table. Click on Layout, Tables and Lines. Select line styles as appropriate.

13. Click on File and Preview to check table setup.

Author-Date Citation with
Microsoft Word for Windows 2.0–6.0

MARGINS

The setting for *APA* papers is one inch on top, bottom and sides. The default setting of Word for Windows is 1.25" left and right and 1.00" top and bottom. You need to adjust the left and right margins. Do not right justify or hyphenate.

1. Click on Format and Page Setup in the Menu Bar. The Page Setup dialog box appears.
2. Click on Margins on the top line. Move the insertion point to the left and right boxes with the mouse.
3. Click on the down arrows in the boxes until 1" appears.
4. Choose Whole Document or This Point Forward, whichever is appropriate, in the Apply to list.
5. Click on OK.

LINE SPACING

APA papers are double spaced throughout.

1. Place the cursor at the beginning of the document.
2. Press Ctrl+2.

PAGINATION

APA papers carry a right justified heading one half inch from the top with the first two or three words of the title in upper and lower case and the page number in Arabic numerals beginning with the first page.

Microsoft Word for Windows 6.0

1. Move the cursor to the top of the first page.
2. Click on View and Header/Footer in the Menu Bar. A Header/Footer toolbar appears in the center of the screen with a dotted box marked Header. The cursor will be inside the box at the left margin.

MICROSOFT WORD WINDOWS

3. Type the first two or three words of the title in upper and lower case. Leave five spaces.

4. Click on the Page Number button with the # sign on the Header tool-bar. The number 1 appears five spaces after your name.

5. Press Ctrl+R to align the header with the right margin.

6. Press Close.

Microsoft Word for Windows 2.0

1. Move the cursor to the top of the first page.

2. Click on View in the Menu Bar and be sure you are in Normal View.

3. Click on View and Header/Footer from the Menu Bar. The Header/Footer dialog box appears. Choose Header and OK. A Header window appears with the cursor at the left margin.

4. Type the first two or three words of the title in upper and lower case. Leave five spaces.

5. Click on the Page Number button with the # sign on the Header tool-bar. The number 1 appears five spaces after the short title.

6. Press Ctrl+R to align header with the right margin.

7. Click on Close.

INDENTION

The *APA* papers are indented five to seven spaces. The Word for Windows default setting is one half inch. The correct tab setting will depend on the font used.

Microsoft Word For Windows 6.0

1. Click on View and Ruler in the Menu Bar. The ruler appears.

2. Click on the box at the left end of the ruler until the symbol L appears.

3. Type an unbroken series of at least 15 characters at the left margin.

4. Click inside the ruler where the fifth, sixth or seventh character is located and release. The new first tab is set.

Microsoft Word for Windows 2.0

1. Click on View and Ruler in the Menu Bar. The ruler appears.

2. Type an unbroken series of at least 15 characters at the left margin.

3. Count 5, 6, or 7 characters from the left margin.

4. Click on the tab marker at the .5" mark on the ruler and drag it to the

fifth, sixth, or seventh character location and release. The new first tab is set.

TITLE PAGE

1. Move the cursor to the top line of the first page.
2. Type at the left margin the words, Running Head:, in upper and lower case, leave two spaces and type an abbreviated title of fewer than 50 characters in all upper case including punctuation and spaces.
3. Center the full title in upper and lower case on the page. Double space if more two or more lines.
4. Center your name in upper and lower case one double space below the title.
5. Center your school name in upper and lower case one double space below your name.

ABSTRACT PAGE

1. Press Ctrl+Enter to begin page 2.
2. Center the word, Abstract, in upper and lower case on the top line under the page number header.
3. Type the abstract, a summary of your paper, in a single paragraph without paragraph indention in fewer than 960 characters including punctuation and spacing.

TEXT

1. Press Ctrl+Enter to begin page 3.
2. Center the title in upper and lower case double spaced at the top.
3. Double space and begin typing text. Do not start a new page when a new section begins.

AUTHOR-DATE CITATIONS

Citations are placed directly in the text. No special keystrokes are necessary. Follow the samples on pages 59–60.

REFERENCES PAGE

1. Click on Insert and Break in the Menu Bar to start a new page. The Break dialog box appears with Page Break selected.
2. Center the word, References, in upper and lower case on the top line. Double space.

3. Type the entries in alphabetical order using the appropriate format shown on pages 62–65 for the type of reference you are citing. First-line of each entry is indented five to seven spaces.

4. Double space within and between entries.

APPENDIXES

1. Click on Insert and Break in the Menu Bar to start a new page. The Break dialog box appears with Page Break selected.

2. Center the word, Appendix, in upper and lower case on the top line. Double space.

3. Center the title of the appendix in upper and lower case.

4. Double space and type the text double spaced with a regular paragraph indent.

TABLES

Microsoft Word for Windows 2.0 and 6.0

1. Move the cursor to the place in the text where the table will be inserted. Leave three blank lines.

2. Type Table 1 flush left in upper and lower case without a period. Double space and type the title, flush left, underlined, in upper and lower case. Extra lines are double spaced flush left.

3. Click on the Insert Table button just above the B, I, U buttons in the upper toolbar. A table box appears.

4. Drag across the columns (vertical) and rows (horizontal) until you have the correct number of cells you need.

5. Move the cursor from cell to cell with the tab or arrow keys. Do not use Enter in the table.

6. Enter headers and data in each cell.

7. Click on Table in the Menu Bar and Select Table.

8. Click on Center button in the standard toolbar and all data in each cell will be centered.

9. Adjust the outside lines of the table by clicking on them. The cursor becomes two vertical lines with arrows pointing left and right. Drag the lines to the left and right edges of the table title.

10. Adjust the width of the columns by clicking on vertical lines and dragging them where you want them.

11. Move the cursor into the table and click on Table and and Center in the toolbar.

5 Endnote Citation

MLA Handbook for Writers of Research Papers, 4th ed. 1995

ENDNOTE CITATION TECHNIQUE

Endnote citation is similar to footnote citation, but it places all the citations in a single, numerically arranged list at the end of the paper. Difficulties arranging footnotes at the bottom of each page are eliminated. Sample endnote formats are shown on pages 91–96.

A superscript endnote number is typed one half space above the line after the last word of the section to be cited like this.[1] The same superscript number appears at the beginning of each endnote on the Notes page. Leave a space between the number and the first letter of the note. Number endnotes consecutively. The first line of each endnote is indented five spaces. Double space within and between each endnote.

A bibliography called, Works Cited, follows the list of notes at the end of the paper. Samples of Works Cited entries are shown on pages 34–38 in **Chapter 3 Author-Page Citation**.

First mention of work must be full and complete entry.

[1] Herbert S. Gershman, The Surrealist Revolution in France (Ann Arbor: U of Michigan P, 1986) 32-33.

Second or later mention of same work. Do not use ibid., or op. cit. Repeat author's last name and page number.

[2] Gershman 49.

More than one work by same author. After first mention add abbreviated title.

[4] Gershman, Study of Life 53.

QUOTATIONS

Quotations of four lines or less are not set off from the text but are placed within double quotation marks. Use single quotation marks for quotations within a short quotation.

For longer quotations, use a comma or colon after the last word of text, double space and type the quotation with no quotation marks. Indent ten spaces from left margin and double space quote. If two or more paragraphs are quoted one after another, indent the first line of each paragraph three more spaces. Use double quotation marks for quotations within a long quotation.

POETRY

Poetry of three lines or less is placed in double quotation marks within the text. Separate lines of poetry which appear in a single line of text by a slash (/) with a space before and after the slash.

For longer poems, use same procedure as for prose. Longer lines may be indented fewer spaces to improve balance.

GENERAL RULES

Periods and commas are placed inside quotation marks. Question marks and exclamation marks not originally in the quotation go outside the quotation marks. Words omitted (ellipses) are shown by three periods with a space between each and a space before the first period and after the last. If a parenthetical reference ends a quoted line, place the period after the reference.

WORKS CITED—BIBLIOGRAPHY

The bibliography is called Works Cited in MLA style. The endnote numbers in your text lead the reader to the list of sources found on the page following the last line of your paper. Entries are alphabetized letter by letter by author's last name, association or title if author's name is not known. Entries are shown single-spaced here to conserve space in this book, **but they must be double-spaced in your paper.**

MLA WORKS CITED SAMPLES

Use the Works Cited samples in **Chapter 3, Author-Page Citation**, pages 34–38.

PRINT SOURCES

BOOKS

BOOK—NO NAMED AUTHOR
[5] Handbook of Pre-Columbian Art (New York: Johnson, 1988) 212-213.

BOOK—ONE AUTHOR
[4] Herbert S. Gershman, The Surrealist Revolution in France (Ann Arbor: U of Michigan P, 1994) 32-33.

BOOK—MULTIPLE AUTHORS
[7] Bernard C. Raffer, Richard Friedman, and Robert A. Baron, New York in Crisis (New York: Harper, 1986) 71-72.

BOOK—SAME AUTHOR—
ADD SHORT TITLE AFTER FIRST MENTION
[4] Gershman, Study of Life 53.

BOOK—EDITED
[12] Herman Melville, Moby Dick, ed. J. P. Small (Boston: Houghton, 1973) 271-274.

BOOK—TRANSLATION
[8] Andre Maurois, Lelia, trans. Gerard Hopkins (New York: Harper, 1954) 14-15.

BOOK—CORPORATE AUTHOR
[6] National Policy Association, Welfare Reform (New York: McGraw, 1992) 74.

MULTIVOLUME WORK—CITING ONE VOLUME ONLY
[8] Richard K. Smith, A History of Religion in the United States, vol. 3 (Chicago: U of Chicago, 1993) 301-303.

MULTIVOLUME WORK—CITING MORE THAN ONE VOLUME
[3] Richard K. Smith, A History of Religion in the United States, 4 vols. (Chicago: U of Chicago, 1993).

GOVERNMENT PUBLICATION

[12] United States, Dept. of Labor, <u>Welfare Reform</u> (Washington: GPO, 1994) 19-21.

DISSERTATION UNPUBLISHED

[25] Robert Samson, "The Influence of Economic Deprivation on Academic Achievement," diss., New York U, 1985, 72.

DISSERTATION—PUBLISHED BY UNIVERSITY MICROFILMS

[13] Lois Garon, <u>Socialist Ideas in the Works of Emile Zola</u>, diss., Brown U, 1985, (Ann Arbor: UMI, 1986) 33-34.

POEMS, ESSAYS, SHORT STORIES, PLAYS IN ANTHOLOGIES

[4] Edgar Allan Poe, "The Raven," <u>Great American Poetry</u>, ed. Richard Johnson (New York: McGraw Hill, 1978) 38-40.

PERIODICALS AND ARTICLES

ARTICLE—IN REFERENCE BOOK—UNSIGNED

[15] "DNA," <u>Encyclopedia Britannica</u>, 1994 ed.

ARTICLE—IN REFERENCE BOOK—SIGNED

[9] Richard Smith, "Color and Light," <u>Encyclopedia Britannica</u>, 1994 ed.

NEWSPAPER ARTICLE—SIGNED

[11] Clifford May, "Religious Frictions Heat Up in Rwanda," <u>New York Times</u> 12 Aug. 1994, late ed.: A1.

MAGAZINE ARTICLE—UNSIGNED

[3] "Making of a Candidate for President," <u>Time</u> 20 July 1984: 40-42.

MAGAZINE ARTICLE—SIGNED

[6] Susan Kuhn, "A New Stock Play in Savings and Loans," <u>Fortune</u> 15 May 1955: 67-72.

EDITORIAL—UNSIGNED

[15] "China's Conscience," editorial, <u>New York Times</u> 19 May 1995, late ed.: A22.

EDITORIAL—SIGNED

[4] Marshall S. Brownhurst, "<u>Rush to Judgement</u>," editorial, <u>Wall Street Journal</u> 5 June 1995: A15.

ABSTRACT IN ABSTRACTS JOURNAL

[11] Josephine K. Frischman, "Analysis of Bias in Selecting Test Times," Journal of Experimental Psychology 98 (1974): 325-331. Psychological Abstracts 80 (1975): item 7321.

ARTICLE IN LOOSELEAF COLLECTION— SOCIAL ISSUES RESOURCES SERIES SIRS

[2] Philip C. Cruver, "Lighting the 21st Century," Futurist Mar. 1990: 29-34. Energy, ed. Eleanor Goldstein, vol. 4. (Boca Raton: SIRS, 1991) art. 84.

ARTICLE IN MICROFICHE COLLECTION—NEWSBANK

[4] Randy Chieper, "Welfare Reform Debates," New York Times 20 Apr. 1994, late ed.: A12, Newsbank: Welfare and Social Problems 17 (1994) fiche 2, grids A9-13.

REVIEW OF BOOK, FILM, PERFORMANCE, OTHER INCLUDE AUTHORS, DIRECTORS, CONDUCTORS, PERFORMERS, OTHERS AS PERTINENT

[6] Janet Maslin, "New Challenges for the Caped Crusader," rev. of Batman Forever, dir. Joel Schumacher, New York Times 16 June 1995, late ed.: C1.

ARTICLE— SIGNED IN JOURNAL WHICH USES ISSUE NUMBERS

[13] Robert Brogdan, "Religious Freedom and School Holidays," Phi Delta Kappan 68 (1984): 700-702.

ARTICLE— SIGNED IN JOURNAL WHICH PAGES ISSUES SEPARATELY

[9] Mary Jones, "Urban Poetry," American Review 13.2 (1987): 66-73.

NON-PRINT SOURCES

TELEVISION OR RADIO PROGRAM

Include show title, program or series title, pertinent actors, directors, producers, network, call letters and city, date

[17] "Pollution in the Desert," narr. Mike Wallace, prod. Jock Fenway, dir. John Brett, Sixty Minutes, CBS WCBS, New York, 6 Mar. 1994.

SOUND RECORDING

Cite first whichever is emphasized: composer, performer, conductor. Then title, artists, audiocassette or LP if not a CD, manufacturer, date or N.D. if unknown.

[5] Andrew Lloyd Webber, <u>Phantom of the Opera</u>, perf. Michael Crawford, Sarah Brightman, and Steve Barton, audiocassette, EMI, 1987.

FILM

Include title, director. Also if pertinent, writers, performers, producers, distributor, year.

[7] <u>Raiders of the Lost Ark</u>, dir. Steven Spielberg, Paramount, 1982.

INTERVIEW—BROADCAST

[9] Phil Gramm, interview with Charlie Rose, <u>Charlie Rose</u>, WNET, New York, 6 May 1994.

INTERVIEW—PERSONAL

[13] Robert Kennedy, personal interview, 11 Jan. 1971.

CD-ROM—DISKETTE—MAGNETIC TAPE

Include author, title, date, database, CD-ROM or diskette or magnetic tape, vendor, electronic publication date.

CD-ROM—PERIODICAL

[20] United States, Dept. of Commerce, "Railroad Tonnage Reports," <u>National Trade Data Bank</u>, CD-ROM, US Dept. of Commerce, Apr. 1994.

CD-ROM—PERIODICAL ALSO PUBLISHED IN PRINT

[17] James Barron, "New York Welfare Programs in Jeopardy," <u>New York Times</u> 8 May 1995, late ed.: C1, <u>New York Times Ondisc</u>, CD-ROM, UMI-Proquest, Nov. 1995.

DISKETTE

[8] Harold J. Bernstein, <u>A History of Crime in America</u>, diskette, (Columbus: U of Ohio P, 1994).

MAGNETIC TAPE

[15] <u>English Poetry Full-Text Database</u>, rel. 2, magnetic tape (Cambridge, Eng.: Chadwyck, 1993).

COMPUTER SERVICES

BRS—Dow Jones News Retrieval—Dialog—Prodigy—OCLC—Compuserve—Nexis—New York Times Online—America Online—Etc.

Include author, title, date, database title, online, computer service, access
date.

DATABASE PUBLISHED PERIODICALLY WITH PRINT AVAILABLE

[3] Frank Rich, "End of an Era in the Middle East,"
New York Times 8 May 1955, late ed.: C1, New York
Times Online, online, Nexis, 15 June 1955.

[5] Studies of Pre-Kindergarten Programs 1983-93
(Urbana: ERIC Clearinghouse on Elementary and Early
Childhood Educ., 1994), ERIC, online, BRS, 28 Oct.
1994.

DATABASE PUBLISHED WITH NO PRINT SOURCE AVAILABLE

[1] Richard Comshaw, "The End of the Bull Market,"
Wall Street Journal, online, Dow Jones News Retrieval,
12 Apr. 1995.

[8] "Civil War," Academic American Encyclopedia,
online, Prodigy, 15 Apr. 1994.

ELECTRONIC JOURNALS—NEWSLETTERS
CONFERENCES—INTERNET

Include author, title, newsletter or journal or conference title, volume or
issue, date, number of pages or *n. pag.* if not paginated, online, computer
network, access date, electronic address preceded with word *available* if
required.

ELECTRONIC JOURNAL

[9] Richard Rabine, "Discussion of Perseveration in
Driving Habits," Psycholoquy (June 1993): 9 pp.,
online, Internet, 11 Nov. 1994.

[6] Richard Lovett, "Teacher Traits," Psycholoquy
(June 1994): 5 pp., online, Internet, 6 Oct. 1993.
Available FTP: Hostname:duke.eduDirectory:pub/harnad/
Psycholoquy/1993.

FILE TRANSFER PROTOCOL

[4] Richard Rabine, "Perseveration in Driving
Habits," Psycholoquy (June 1993) FTP: Hostname
duke.eduDirectory:pub/harnad/Psycholoquy/1993.Volume.4.
File psycoloquy.93.4.13.base-rate.12.rabine.

MLA ENDNOTE SAMPLES

E-MAIL

5 Richard Lovett, "Discussion of Teacher Traits," <u>Psychololquy</u> (June 1993) E-mail: psych@ducc Message: Get psyc 93-xxxx.

ELECTRONIC TEXT

Include author, title, print publication date, online, electronic text repository, computer network, access date, electronic address preceded with word *available* if required

12 Emily Bronte, <u>Collected Poems</u>, ed. Joseph Schmidt, (London: Oxford UP, 1981). online. U of California Lib. Internet. 12 Oct. 1995. Available: ocf.berkeley.edu/OCF On-line Library/Poetry

SAMPLE *MLA* FIRST TEXT PAGE (TITLE PAGE) WITH ENDNOTE CITATION

½"

Quarles   1

1"

3 spaces

Roger P. Quarles

Professor Swarthouse

Sociology 112

9 September 1995   Double space

Center title   Workfare Programs in Three States

President Clinton pledged an "end to welfare as we know it"

as part of the 1992 election campaign. However, the

administration has been unable to get the Congress to act on the

suggested reforms and, as a result, the states have proposed a

wide range of experimental initiatives.[1] When Congress passed

1"   the Jobs Opportunities and Basic Skills Program (JOBS) in 1988,   1"

it gave states matching funds to develop programs. Wisconsin,

Delaware, and California are among the states which have begun

Endnote superscript

workfare programs.[2]

However, the picture is not altogether sanguine. Some

critics of the workfare concept including Gilbert claim that

workfare will increase welfare costs and simultaneously increase

the numbers of homeless person.[3] There are arguments that

despite the faults of the old AFDC program fifty percent of

recipients are off welfare within two years.

Others state that a lack of funds for job training and child

care will make workfare programs impossible to maintain.

Wisconsin's workfare program, often cited as a model, has not

worked well for the clients or the employers say its critics.[4]

Nevertheless, there have been some important gains in a number of

areas. Although clearly not a majority, a number of recipients

1"

SAMPLE *MLA* NOTES PAGE

Notes   Double space ←

**Endnote
superscript** →

1 Susan Kellam, "Welfare Experiments: Are States Leading the Way Toward National Reform?" <u>Congressional Quarterly Researcher</u> 16 Sept. 1994: 795-796.

2 Kellam 797.

3 Neil Gilbert, "Why the New Workfare Won't Work," <u>Commentary</u> May 1994: 47.

4 Mickey Kaus, "Tough Enough: A Promising Start on Welfare Reform," <u>The New Republic</u> 25 Apr. 1994: 23.

5 Karl Robinson, and Bernard R. Politcheck, <u>The Politics of Welfare Reform</u> (New York: McGraw Hill, 1994) 213-214.

6 Gilbert 47.

8 Roberta J. Carlson, <u>The Dream and the Dilemma: Welfare in America</u> (New York: Macmillan, 1994) 212-213.

←— 1" —→

9 United States, Dept. of Health and Human Services, <u>Survey of Job Training Programs</u> (Washington: GPO, 1992) 34-37.

Space

10 Carlson 217.

11 Miriam Schwartz, "The Role of the Mother in AFDC Families," <u>Consulting Psychology Journal: Practice and Research</u> 45.4 (1993): 28

12 Phillip R. Bernstein, Charles D. Delanson, and Paul Connelson, "Attitudinal Changes in Mothers Engaged in Job Training," <u>Journal of Applied Psychology</u> 78 (1993): 453.

13 Schwartz 29.

14 Ruth Conniff, "Cutting the Lifeline: The Real Welfare Fraud," <u>The Progressive</u> Feb. 1992: 27.

15 Carlson 215.

←— 1" —→

SAMPLE *MLA* WORKS CITED PAGE

Works Cited

Bernstein, Phillip R., Charles D. Delanson, and Paul Connelson.
    "Attitudinal Changes in Mothers Engaged in Job Training."
    Journal of Applied Psychology 78 (1993): 452-457.

Carlson, Roberta J. The Dream and the Dilemma: Welfare in
    America. New York: Macmillan, 1994.

Conniff, Ruth. "Cutting the Lifeline: The Real Welfare Fraud."
    The Progressive Feb. 1992: 25-28

Cowan, Noah. "The Big Lie About Workfare." Utne Reader May-
    June 1992: 28-29.

Gilbert, Neil. "Why the New Workfare Won't Work." Commentary
    May 1994: 47.

Kaus, Mickey. "Tough Enough: A Promising Start on Welfare
    Reform." The New Republic 25 Apr. 1994: 22-23.

Kellam, Susan. "Welfare Experiments: Are States Leading the Way
    Toward National Reform?" Congressional Quarterly Researcher
    16 Sept.1994: 795-796.

Robinson, Karl, and Bernard R. Politcheck. The Politics of
    Welfare Reform. New York: McGraw Hill, 1994.

Schwartz, Miriam. "The Role of the Mother in AFDC Families."
    Consulting Psychology Journal: Practice and Research 45.4
    (1993): 27-29.

United States. Dept. of Health and Human Services. Survey of
    Jobs Training Programs. Washington: GPO, 1992.

"Workfare Debate Heats Up in Legislatures." Washington Post 21
    Aug. 1993: A3.

1" ← →   ← 1" →

1"

Word Processing the Paper

Locate the instructions for your word processor in this section by using the tabs on the side margins. Complete instructions and computer keystrokes for page layouts and special formats required by the *MLA Handbook for Writers of Research Papers* are shown.

Endnote Citation with
WordPerfect 4.2–5.1–6.0 for DOS

Follow the Instructions for Author-Page Word Processing in Chapter 3. Except for Endnote Citation Technique.

ENDNOTE CITATION

WordPerfect will automatically number endnotes and place them at the end of the paper.

1. Move the cursor after the word or phrase you wish to cite without a space.
2. Press Ctrl+F7 and 3 for Endnote. (2 for Endnote in **WordPerfect 4.2–5.1**).
3. Press C for Create.
4. Press Tab to indent the endnote five spaces. Leave a space after the endnote number and type the endnote using the correct format on pages 91–96 for the type of reference you are citing.
5. Press C for create and the endnote number appears at the top of the screen.
6. Press F7 to return to your paper.

Continue the process for the following endnotes. Endnote numbers will be in superscript.

To Edit an Endnote:

1. Press E for Edit instead of C for create and the number of the endnote to be corrected.
2. Press F7 when correction is completed.

To Delete an Endnote:

1. Move the cursor to just before the endnote number in the text and press Delete and Y.

Endnote Citation with
Microsoft Word 5.0–6.0 for DOS

**Follow the Instructions for Author-Page Word Processing in Chapter 3.
Except for Endnote Citations Technique.**

ENDNOTE CITATION

Microsoft Word will automatically number endnotes and place them at the
end of the paper.

1. Press Esc, F, D, L for Layout, and E for End.

2. Press Enter.

3. Move the cursor immediately after the phrase or sentence you wish to
   cite without a space.

4. Press Esc, F, F for Footnote, and Enter. Two diamonds appear with the
   number 1 for the first endnote between them. With the cursor over
   the endnote number, press tab to indent five spaces, press the right
   arrow key once and the spacebar to move the cursor one space to the
   right of the number.

5. Type the endnote using the appropriate format shown on pages 91–96
   for the type of reference you are citing.

6. Press Esc, J for Jump, F for Footnote, and the cursor will return to the
   endnote reference number in the text.

7. Endnote numbers appear as superscripts like this.[1] With the highlight
   over the number in the endnote and each time the cursor jumps back
   to the endnote number in the text, press Alt and + +. Then use the
   arrow key to resume typing.

Endnote Citation with

WordPerfect for Windows 5.2–6.0

Follow the Instructions for Author-Page Word Processing in Chapter 3. Except for Endnote Citations Technique.

ENDNOTE CITATIONS

WordPerfect for Windows will automatically number endnotes and place them at the end of the paper.

1. Move the cursor immediately after the phrase or sentence you wish to cite without a space.
2. Click on Layout, Endnote, and Create in the Menu Bar. An Endnote window and button bar appears with the number 1. at the left margin.
3. Type the endnote using the correct format shown on pages 91–96 for the type of reference you are citing.
4. Click on Close. The cursor will return to your text. When you create the next endnote, WordPerfect will automatically double space between endnotes.

To Edit an Endnote:

1. Click on Layout, Endnote and Edit in the Menu Bar. The Edit Endnote dialog box appears.
2. Type the number of the Endnote you want to edit.

To delete an endnote:

1. Select the endnote number of the endnote you want to delete in the text. Press Delete. All endnotes will be renumbered.

WORDPERFECT WINDOWS

Endnote Citation with
Microsoft Word for Windows 2.0–6.0

Follow the Instructions for Author-Page Word Processing in Chapter 3. Except for Endnote Citations Technique.

ENDNOTE CITATIONS

Word for Windows will automatically number endnotes and place them at the end of the paper.

Microsoft Word for Windows 6.0

1. Click on View and make sure you are in Normal View.
2. Move the cursor immediately after the phrase or sentence you wish to cite without a space.
3. Click on Insert and Footnote in the Menu Bar. The Footnote and Endnote dialog box appears with AutoNumber selected.
4. Click on Endnote and OK. The Endnote window appears with the number 1 with the cursor just to its right at the left margin.
5. Move the cursor with the left arrow key to left of the the number and press Tab to indent the first line of the note.
6. Move the cursor now one space to the right of the number.
7. Type the endnote using the appropriate format shown on pages 91–96 for the type of reference you are citing. Double space within the endnote. Follow the same procedure for the next endnote. Double space between endnotes.
8. To view an existing endnote double click its endnote number.
9. Press Close to close the endnote window.
10. After the last line of text press Ctrl+Enter to start a new page.
11. Center the word, Notes, in upper and lower case on the top line and double space.

12. Press the commands to print. Endnotes will be printed at the end of the paper.

Microsoft Word for Windows 2.0

1. Click on View and be sure you are in Normal View.
2. Move the cursor immediately after the phrase or sentence you wish to cite without a space.
3. Click on Insert and Footnote in the Menu Bar. The Footnote dialog box appears with Auto-Number and Footnote selected.
4. Click on Options. The Footnote Options dialog box appears.
5. Click on Place At: and drag down to End of Document.
6. Click on OK. The Footnote Dialog box appears again.
7. Click on OK. The Footnote window appears with the number 1 with the cursor just to the its right at the left margin.
8. Move the cursor with the left arrow key to left of the the number and press Tab to indent the first line of the note.
9. Move the cursor now one space to the right of the number.
10. Type the endnote using the appropriate format shown on pages 91–96 for the type of reference you are citing. Double space within the endnote. Follow the same procedure for the next endnote. Double space between endnotes.
11. Press F6. The endnote window will remain open and the cursor will jump back to your text.
12. Press F6 again and the cursor will jump to the endnote window.
13. Click on Close and the cursor will return to the text.
14. After the last line of text press Ctrl+Enter to start a new page.
15. Center the word, Notes, in upper and lower case on the top line and double space.
16. Press the commands to print. Endnotes will be printed at the end of the paper.

To edit an endnote:

Microsoft Word for Windows 6.0

1. Double click on the endnote number in the text.
2. Edit the endnote and click on Close.

M
I
C
R
O W
S I
O N
F D
T O
   W
W S
O
R
D

105

Microsoft Word for Windows 2.0

1. Press F5 twice. The Go to dialog box appears.
2. Type f space and the endnote number.
3. Edit the endnote and click on Close.

To delete an endnote:

1. Select the reference mark and press Delete

⑥ Footnote Citation

A Manual for Writers of Term Papers, Theses and Dissertations, 5th ed.

FOOTNOTE CITATION TECHNIQUE

These styles are based on the *Chicago Manual of Style* published by the University of Chicago. This book has long been a standard reference for writers of scholarly papers.

Footnote citation enables the reader to identify references with a glance at the bottom of the page. Footnotes are usually required in theses and dissertations, particularly in the humanities.

A superscript footnote number is typed one half space above the line after the last word of the section to be cited, like this.[2] The same superscript number appears at the beginning of the footnote at the bottom of the page.

Footnotes are indented 6–8 spaces. There is no space between the superscript number and the entry. Second and following lines are single spaced and not indented. Double space between footnotes. Footnotes are numbered consecutively beginning with number one.

First mention of work must be a full and complete entry.

    [1]Herbert S. Gershman, The Surrealist Revolu-
tion in France (Ann Arbor: University of Michigan
Press, 1986), 32–33.

Second mention of same work with no intervening entries. Use Latin abbreviation, Ibid., meaning "in the same place." and the page number(s).

    [2]Ibid., 49.

Second or later mention of same work with intervening entries. Repeat author's last name and page number.

    [2]Gershman, 51.

FOOTNOTE CITATION TECHNIQUE

Second or later mention of the author when more than one work by the same author will be cited. Use the author's name and add an abbreviated title.

³Gershman, <u>Surrealist Revolution</u>, 53.

QUOTATIONS

Prose

Quotations of three lines or less are not set off from the text but are placed within double quotation marks. Use single quotation marks for quotations within a short quotation.

For longer quotations, use a comma or colon after the last word of text, double space twice and type the quotation with no quotation marks. Indent four spaces from left margin and single space quote. Indent four more spaces to set off the beginning of paragraphs. Use double quotation marks for quotations within a long quotation.

Poetry

Short quotations of fewer than three lines are inserted directly in the text with quotation marks at the beginning and end. Two lines of poetry which appear on one line of text are separated by a slash (/) with a space before and after.

Quotations two or more lines long should be set off from the text and typed as in the original. Center on the page without quotation marks. Long lines that cannot be centered should be indented four spaces with left-over words indented four more spaces.

GENERAL RULES

Periods and commas are placed inside quotation marks. Question marks and exclamation marks not originally in the quotation go outside the quotation marks. Words omitted (ellipses) are shown by three periods with a space between each and a space before the first period and after the last.

BOOKS

BOOK—NO NAMED AUTHOR

[1]<u>Handbook of Pre-Columbian Art</u> (New York: Johnson, 1988), 212-213.

BOOK—ONE AUTHOR

[2]Herbert S. Gershman, <u>The Surrealist Revolution in France</u> (Ann Arbor: University of Michigan Press, 1986), 32-33.

BOOK—MULTIPLE AUTHORS

[4]Bernard C. Raffer, Richard Friedman, and Robert A. Baron, <u>New York in Crisis</u> (New York: Harper, 1986), 71-72.

BOOK—EDITED

[3]Herman Melville, <u>Moby Dick</u>, ed. J. P. Small (Boston: Houghton, 1973), 11-12.

BOOK—TRANSLATION

[2]Andre Maurois, <u>Lelia</u>, trans. Gerard Hopkins (New York: Harper, 1954), 89-90.

BOOK—ASSOCIATION AUTHOR

[6]National Policy Association, <u>Welfare Reform</u> (New York: McGraw, 1992), 128-129.

POEMS, ESSAYS, SHORT STORIES, PLAYS IN ANTHOLOGIES

[4]Edgar Allan Poe, "The Raven," in <u>Great American Poetry</u>, ed. Richard Johnson (New York: McGraw, 1978), 38-40.

DISSERTATION

[25]Robert Samson, "The Influence of Economic Deprivation on Academic Achievement" (Ph.D. diss., New York University, 1985), 72.

GOVERNMENT PUBLICATION

[8]Department of Labor, <u>Labor Relations in the Steel Industry</u> ([Washington, D.C.]: U.S. Department of Labor, 1995), 212.

FOOTNOTE CITATION

PERIODICALS AND ARTICLES

ARTICLE IN REFERENCE BOOK—UNSIGNED

[15]<u>Encyclopedia Americana</u>, 1994 ed., s.v. "DNA."

ARTICLE IN REFERENCE BOOK—SIGNED

[9]<u>Encyclopedia Brittanica</u>, 1994 ed., s.v. "Color and Light," by Richard Smith.

NEWSPAPER ARTICLE—SIGNED

[12]Clifford May, "Religious Frictions Heat Up in Rwanda,"<u>New York Times</u>, 12 August 1994, late ed., Sec. A, p.2.

MAGAZINE ARTICLE—UNSIGNED

[6]"Making of a Candidate for President," <u>Time</u>, 20 July 1984, 40.

MAGAZINE ARTICLE—SIGNED

[21]Susan Kuhn, "A New Stock Play in Savings and Loans," <u>Fortune</u>, 15 May 1995, 67–72.

ARTICLE—SIGNED IN JOURNAL WITH VOLUME NUMBERS

[18]Robert Brogdan, "Religious Freedom and School Holidays," <u>Phi Delta Kappan</u> 68 (May 1993): 700–722.

ARTICLE—SIGNED IN JOURNAL WITH VOLUME AND ISSUE NUMBERS

[9]Mary Jones, "Urban Poetry," <u>American Review</u> 13, no. 2 (1987): 66–67.

ARTICLE IN LOOSELEAF COLLECTION— SOCIAL ISSUES RESOURCES SERIES

[12]Philip C. Cruver, "Lighting in the 21st Century," <u>Futurist</u>, March 1990, 29–34. in <u>Energy</u>, ed. Eleanor Goldstein, vol. 4. (Boca Raton: SIRS, 1990). Article 84.

ARTICLE IN MICROFICHE COLLECTION—NEWSBANK

[31]Randy Chieper, "Welfare Reform Debates," <u>New York Times</u>, 20 April 1994, late ed.: A12. in <u>Newsbank: Welfare and Social Problems</u> 17 (1994): fiche 2, grids A9–13.

REVIEW—BOOK, FILM, PERFORMANCE

[7]Janet Maslin, "New Challenges for the Caped Crusader," review of <u>Batman Forever</u>, directed by Joel Schumacher, in <u>New York Times</u>, 16 June 1995, late ed.: C1.

TELEVISION OR RADIO PROGRAM
Include writers, producers, directors, others as pertinent

[11]"Pollution in the Desert," narrated by Mike Wallace, produced by Jack Fenway, directed by John Brett, <u>Sixty Minutes</u>, CBS, WCBS, New York, 6 March 1984.

FILM
Include title, director. Also if pertinent, writers, performers, producers, distributor, year

[19]<u>Raiders of the Lost Ark</u>, directed by Steven Spielberg, Paramount, 1982.

INTERVIEW
[29]Richard Cole, interview by author, 3 February 1994, New York, tape recording, New York University Library, New York.

PORTABLE DATABASES

CD—ROM
[17]James Barron, "New York Transit in Jeopardy," <u>New York Times</u>, 8 May 1995, late ed.: C1. <u>New York Times Ondisc</u>, CD-ROM, UMI, Proquest, November 1995.

ONLINE DATABASES

COMPUTER SERVICE—
BRS, DIALOG, COMPUSERV, NEXIS, AMERICA ONLINE, ETC.
[6]<u>Studies of Pre-Kindergarten Programs 1983-93</u>, Urbana: ERIC Clearinghouse on Elementary and Early Childhood Education, 1994. Dialog, ERIC, ED 321 214.

COMPUTER NETWORKS—INTERNET
[14]Richard Rabine, "Perseveration in Driving Habits," <u>Psychology</u> (June 1993): 9 pp., online, Internet, 11 November 1994.

FILE TRANSFER PROTOCOL—FTP
[4]Richard Rabine, "Perseveration in Driving Habits," <u>Psychology</u> (June 1993) FTP: Hostname duke.eduDirectory: pub/harnad/Psychology/1993.Volume.4File psycoloquy.93.4.13.base-rate.12.rabine.

ONLINE—E-MAIL
[9]Lovett, Richard, "Discussion of Teacher Traits," <u>Psychology</u> (June 1993) E-mail: psych@ducc Message: Get psyc 93-xxxx.

FOOTNOTE CITATION

BOOKS

BOOK—NO NAMED AUTHOR

Handbook of Pre-Columbian Art. New York: Johnson 1988.

BOOK—ONE AUTHOR

Gershman, Herbert S. The Surrealist Revolution in France.
    Ann Arbor: University of Michigan Press, 1986.

BOOK—MULTIPLE AUTHORS

Raffer, Bernard C., Richard Friedman, and Robert A.
    Baron. New York in Crisis. New York: Harper, 1986.

BOOK—EDITED

Melville, Herman. Moby Dick. Edited by J.P. Small.
    Boston: Houghton, 1973.

BOOK—TRANSLATION

Maurois, Andre. Lelia. Translated by Gerard Hopkins.
    New York: Harper, 1954.

BOOK—ASSOCIATION AUTHOR

National Policy Association. Welfare Reform. New York:
    McGraw, 1992.

POEMS, ESSAYS, SHORT STORIES, PLAYS IN ANTHOLOGIES

Poe, Edgar Allan. "The Raven." In Great American
    Poetry. edited by Richard Johnson. New York:
    McGraw, 1978.

DISSERTATION

Samson, Robert. "The Influence of Economic Deprivation
    on Academic Achievement." Ph. D. diss., New York
    University, 1985.

GOVERNMENT PUBLICATION

U.S. Department of Labor. Labor Relations in the Steel
    Industry. [Washington, D.C.]: U.S. Department of
    Labor, 1995.

PERIODICALS AND ARTICLES

ARTICLE IN REFERENCE BOOK—UNSIGNED

Encyclopedia Americana. 1994 ed. S.v. "DNA."

ARTICLE IN REFERENCE BOOK—SIGNED

<u>Encyclopedia Brittanica</u>. 1994 ed. S.v. "Color and
    Light," by Richard Smith.

NEWSPAPER ARTICLE—SIGNED

May, Clifford. "Religious Frictions Heat Up in Rwanda."
    <u>New York Times</u>, 12 August 1994, Late ed. Sec A,
    p.2.

MAGAZINE ARTICLE—UNSIGNED

"Making of a Candidate for President." <u>Time</u>, 20 July
    1984, 40.

MAGAZINE ARTICLE—SIGNED

Kuhn, Susan. "A New Stock Play in Savings and Loans."
    <u>Fortune</u>, 15 May 1995, 67-72.

ARTICLE—SIGNED IN JOURNAL WITH VOLUME NUMBERS

Brogdan, Robert. "Religious Freedom and School Holi-
    days." <u>Phi Delta Kappan</u> 68 (May 1993): 700-722.

ARTICLE—
SIGNED IN JOURNAL WITH VOLUME AND ISSUE NUMBERS

Jones, Mary. "Urban Poetry." <u>American Review</u> 13, no. 2
    (1987): 66-73.

ARTICLE IN LOOSELEAF COLLECTION—
SOCIAL ISSUES RESOURCES SERIES

Cruver, Philip C. "Lighting the 21st Century."
    <u>Futurist</u>, March 1990, 29-34. In <u>Energy</u>. Edited
    by Eleanor Goldstein. Vol. 4. (Boca Raton: SIRS,
    1990). Article No. 84.

ARTICLE IN MICROFICHE COLLECTION—NEWSBANK

Chieper, Randy. "Welfare Reform Debates." <u>New York
    Times</u>, 20 April 1994, Late ed.: A12. In <u>News-
    bank: Welfare and Social Problems</u> 17 (1994):
    fiche 2, grids A9-13.

REVIEW—BOOK, FILM, PERFORMANCE

Maslin, Janet. "New Challenges for the Caped
    Crusader." Review of <u>Batman Forever</u>, directed by
    Joel Schumacher. In <u>New York Times</u>, 16 June
    1995, Late ed.: C1.

TELEVISION OR RADIO PROGRAM

Include writers, producers, directors, others as pertinent.

"Pollution in the Desert." Narrated by Mike Wallace. Produced by John Brett. <u>Sixty Minutes</u>. CBS. WCBS. New York. 6 March 1994.

FILM

Include title, director. Also if pertinent, writers, performers, producers, distributor, year.

<u>Raiders of the Lost Ark</u>. Directed by Steven Spielberg. Paramount, 1982.

INTERVIEW

Cole, Richard. Interview by author, 3 February 1994, New York. Tape recording. New York University Library. New York.

PORTABLE DATABASES

CD-ROM

Barron, James. "New York Transit in Jeopardy." <u>New York Times</u>, 8 May 1995, Late ed.: C1. <u>New York Times Ondisc</u>. CD-ROM. UMI. Proquest. November 1995.

ONLINE DATABASES

COMPUTER SERVICES—
BRS, DIALOG, COMPUSERV, NEXIS, AMERICA ONLINE, ETC.

<u>Studies of Pre-Kindergarten Programs 1983-93</u>. Urbana: ERIC Clearinghouse on Elementary and Early Childhood Education, 1994. Dialog. ERIC. ED 321 214.

COMPUTER NETWORKS—INTERNET

Rabine, Richard. "Perseveration in Driving Habits." <u>Psychoquy</u> (June 1993): 9 pp. Online. Internet. 11 November 1994.

FILE TRANSFER PROTOCOL—FTP

Rabine, Richard. "Perseveration in Driving Habits." <u>Psychoquy</u> (June 1993) FTP: Hostname duke.eduDirectory:pub/harnad/Psycholoquy/1993.Volume.4 File psycoloquy.93.4.13.base-rate.12.rabine.

E-MAIL

Lovett, Richard. "Discussion of Teacher Traits." <u>Psychoquy</u> (June 1993) E-mail: psych@ducc Message: Get psyc 93-xxxx.

SAMPLE *CHICAGO MANUAL OF STYLE* TITLE PAGE

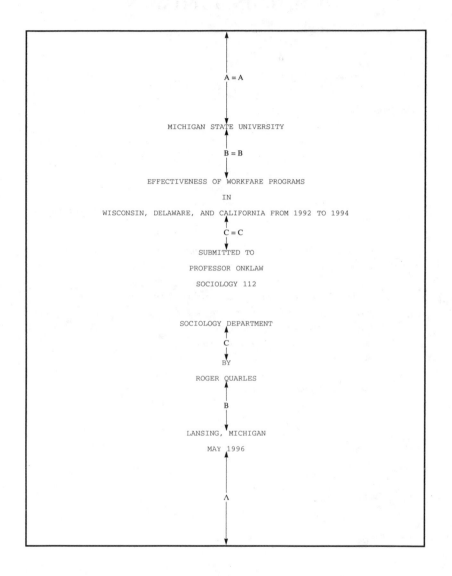

A = A

MICHIGAN STATE UNIVERSITY

B = B

EFFECTIVENESS OF WORKFARE PROGRAMS

IN

WISCONSIN, DELAWARE, AND CALIFORNIA FROM 1992 TO 1994

C = C

SUBMITTED TO

PROFESSOR ONKLAW

SOCIOLOGY 112

SOCIOLOGY DEPARTMENT

C

BY

ROGER QUARLES

B

LANSING, MICHIGAN

MAY 1996

A

SAMPLE *CHICAGO MANUAL OF STYLE* TEXT PAGE
WITH FOOTNOTE CITATION

Regular pages
numbered at top center   4   Double space

President Clinton pledged an "end to welfare as we know it" as part of the 1992 election campaign. However, the administration has been unable to get the Congress to act on the suggested reforms and, as a result, the states have proposed a wide range of experimental initiatives.[1] When Congress passed the Jobs Opportunities and Basic Skills Program (JOBS) in 1988, it gave states matching funds to develop programs. Wisconsin, Delaware, and California are among the states which have begun workfare programs.[2]

Footnote superscript

However, the picture is not altogether sanguine. Some critics of the workfare concept including Gilbert claim that workfare will increase welfare costs and simultaneously increase the numbers of homeless persons.[3] There are arguments that despite the faults of the old AFDC program fifty percent of recipients are off welfare within two years.

Others state that a lack of funds for job training and child care will make workfare programs impossible to maintain. Wisconsin's workfare program, often cited as a model, has not worked well for the clients or the employers say its critics.[4] Nevertheless, there have been some important gains and a

Double space

Double space

1"

1"

1"

---

[1]Susan Kellam, "Welfare Experiments: Are States Leading the Way Toward National Reform?" <u>Congressional Quarterly Researcher</u>, 16 September 1994, 795-796.

[2]Ibid., 799.

[3]Neil Gilbert, "Why the New Workfare Won't Work," <u>Commentary</u>, May 1994, 47.

[4]Mickey Kaus, "Tough Enough: A Promising Start on Welfare Reform," <u>The New Republic</u>, 25 April 1994, 22-23.

1"

SAMPLE *CHICAGO MANUAL OF STYLE* BIBLIOGRAPHY PAGE

2"   ← First page of new sections only

BIBLIOGRAPHY

← Double space twice

Bernstein, Phillip R., Charles D. Delanson, and Paul Connelson. "Attitudinal Changes in Mothers Engaged in Job Training." Journal of Applied Psychology 78 (1993): 453-457.

Double space →

Carlson, Roberta J. The Dream and the Dilemma: Welfare in America. New York: Macmillan, 1994.

Conniff, Ruth. "Cutting the Lifeline: The Real Welfare Fraud." The Progressive, February 1992, 25-28.

Cowan, Noah. "The Big Lie About Workfare." Utne Reader, May-June 1992, 28-29.

Gilbert, Neil. "Why the New Workfare Won't Work." Commentary, May 1994, 47.

← 1" → Kaus, Mickey. "Tough Enough: A Promising Start on Welfare Reform." The New Republic, 25 April 1995, 22-23.   ← 1" →

Kellam, Susan. "Welfare Experiments: Are the States Leading the Way Toward National Reform?" Congressional Quarterly Researcher, 16 September 1994, 795-797.

Single space →

Mitchell, Allison. "Clinton and Dole Present Programs to Alter Welfare." New York Times, 1 August 1995, Late ed. Sec A, p. 1.

Robinson, Karl, and Bernard R. Politcheck. The Politics of Welfare Reform. New York: McGraw Hill, 1994.

Schwartz, Miriam. "The Role of the Mother in AFDC Families." Consulting Psychology Journal: Practice and Research, 45, no. 4 (1993):27-29.

U.S. Department of Health and Human Services. Survey of Jobs Training Programs. [Washington, D.C.]: U.S. Department of Health and Human Services, 1992.

"Workfare Debate Heats Up in Legislatures." Washington Post, 21 August 1993, Sec. A, p.3.

Zelans, Charles. War on Poverty. Chicago: Presidio, 1995.

First page of new sections numbered at bottom center → 12

1"

Word Processing the Paper

Locate the instructions for your word processor in this section by using the tabs on the side margins. Complete instructions and and computer keystrokes for page layouts and special formats required by *The Chicago Manual of Style* are shown.

Footnote Citation with
WordPerfect for DOS 4.2–6.0

MARGINS

The setting for *Chicago Manual of Style* papers is one inch on top, bottom and sides. The is is the default setting for WordPerfect. You need to adjust the top margin now and later the bottom margin to one half inch to properly place the page numbers. Bottom margin instructions will be found under Pagination. Do not right justify or hyphenate.

WordPerfect 6.0.

1. Move the cursor to the top of the first page.
2. Press Shift+F8. The Format menu appears.
3. Press M for Margins T for Top and type .5″.
4. Press F7 three times.

WordPerfect 4.2–5.1

1. Move the cursor to the top of the first page.
2. Press Shift+F8. The Format menu appears.
3. Press P for Page and M for Margins. The cursor will move to Top.
4. Type .5″.
5. Press F7, F7.

LINE SPACING

Chicago Manual of Style papers are double spaced except for footnotes and bibliography entries which are single spaced.

1. Move the cursor to the top of the first page.
2. Press Shift+F8, L for Line and S for Spacing.
3. Press 1 for single and 2 for double spacing.
4. Press F7 twice in 4.2–5.0 and three times in 6.0.

PAGINATION

Chicago Manual of Style papers are numbered consecutively in Arabic from first page of text to last page of bibliography at the top center of each page except for first pages of new sections such as bibliography and chapters which are numbered at the the bottom center of each page.

Preliminary pages such as the table of contents and dedication are numbered at the bottom center in small Roman numerals beginning with ii. because you count, but do not number the title page. The table of contents is usually numbered, ii.

Regular Pages

WordPerfect 6.0

1. Move the cursor to the top of the first page
2. Press Shift+F8. The Format menu appears.
3. Press P for Page and N for Page Numbering. The Page Numbering dialog box appear.
4. Press P for Position. The Page Number Position dialog box appears.
5. Press 2 for numbering at top center and press F7 four times.
6. Press Shift+F7 and V for View to see the page number in preview.
7. Press F7, F7 to return to your paper.

WordPerfect 4.2–5.1

1. Move the cursor to the top of the first page.
2. Press Shift+F8. The Format menu appears.

3. Press P for Page and N for Page Numbering.

4. Press P for Position and 2 which corresponds with top center and F7.

5. Press Shift+F7 and V for View to check position of the page numbers in preview.

6. Press F7, F7 to return to your paper.

First Pages of New Sections

The easiest way to handle the first pages of new sections is to allow Word-Perfect to number all pages at the top. Print the paper. Locate the first pages of new sections and reformat to place page numbers at bottom center.

1. Go back to Margins instruction.

2. Scroll to the top of the of the first page of the first new section such as Bibliography. Note the page number at the lower left of the screen.

3. Change the Top margin setting to 1"

4. Change the Bottom margin setting to .5"

5. Follow the instructions for Pagination except change the Position to bottom center.

6. Press Shift+F7 and 2 to print only this page.

7. Repeat for each page of a new section.

Preliminary Pages

WordPerfect 6.0

1. Press P for Page, N for Numbering, P for Position, 6 for Bottom Center and F7.

2. Press N for Number, M for Method and arrow down to Lower Roman. Type ii for Table of Contents.

WordPerfect 4.2–5.1

1. WordPerfect 4.2 and 5.1 will not print small Roman numerals. Use a typewriter to number these pages.

INDENTION

Chicago Manual of Style papers are indented six to eight spaces. The Word-Perfect default setting is one half inch. The correct tab setting will depend on the font used.

WordPerfect 4.2–5.1

1. Move the cursor to the top of the first page.
2. Press Shift+F8, L and T for Tab Set. The Tab ruler appears.
3. Count six to eight characters from the left margin to locate the new first tab position in inches on the ruler.
4. Press the left or right arrow keys to position the new first tab stop and press L to set the new first tab.
5. Move the cursor to the old first tab and press Delete.
6. Press F7 three times to return to your text.

TITLE PAGE

1. Move cursor to the top line of the first page.
2. Use your college or school style exactly. Otherwise, center and double space in all upper case: name of school, title of paper, your name, course, teacher's name, and date. The title page is not numbered.

FOOTNOTE CITATIONS

WordPerfect will automatically number footnotes and place them at the bottom of each page.

1. Move the cursor after the word or phrase you wish to cite without a space.
2. Press Ctrl+F7.
3. Press F for Footnote and C for Create.
4. Type the footnote using the correct formats shown on pages 109–111 for the type of reference you are citing.
5. Press F7 to return to your paper.
6. Press Shift+F7 and V for View to preview.
7. Continue the process for following footnotes. The separation line between text and footnotes will automatically appear. Footnote numbers will be in superscript. Single space within footnotes but double space between footnotes.

To Edit a Footnote:

1. Press Ctrl+F7.
2. Press E for Edit instead of C above and the number of the footnote to be corrected.
3. Press F7 when correction is completed.

To Delete a Footnote:

1. Move the cursor to just before the footnote number in the text and press Delete and Y.

BIBLIOGRAPHY

1. Press Ctrl+Enter to start a new page.
2. Center the word, BIBLIOGRAPHY, in upper case thirteen lines down from the top of the page.
3. Double space twice and type entries in alphabetical order using the correct format shown on pages 112–114 for the type of reference you are citing.
4. First line of each entry begins at left margin with following lines single spaced and indented 6–8 spaces.
5. Double space between entries. The first page of the bibliography section is numbered at the bottom center.

TABLES

WordPerfect 6.0

1. Move the cursor to the place in the text where the table will be inserted. Leave three blank lines.
2. Type at the margin Table 1.—And the Title Just Like This in upper and lower case and center. Extra lines are centered and single spaced.
3. Press Alt+F7. The Columns/Table dialog box appears.
4. Press T for Tables and C for Create. The Create Table dialog box appears.
5. Type in number of columns. Arrow down, and type in number of rows and press Enter, Enter. The table appears.
6. Press F7, F7 to return to your text.
7. Type headers at the top of each column and enter data in each cell using tab and arrow keys. Center the data and header titles each cell.
8. Press Alt+F7, T, E for Edit, and Enter.
9. Press Ctrl+arrow keys to reduce width of each cell to slightly larger than the header.
10. Press 4 for Table and P for Position. Arrow down to Center and Press Enter.
11. Press F7. Table will be centered on your text page. Adjust title so it

is flush with the upper left margin of the table. Leave three blank lines and resume typing.

WordPerfect 4.2–5.1

1. Move the cursor to the place in the text where the table will be inserted. Leave three blank lines.

2. Type at the margin Table 1.—And the Title Just Like This in upper and lower case and center. Extra lines are centered and single spaced.

3. Press Alt+F7, T for Tables and C for Create. The Number of Columns prompt appears.

4. Type the number of columns (vertical) you need and press Enter. The Number of Rows prompt appears. Type the number of rows (horizontal) you need and press Enter. The table appears.

5. Press F7 to return to your text and type the header titles in the first row of the table. Enter data in each cell using Tab and arrow keys. Center the data and header titles in each box.

6. Press Alt+F7 to edit the table. Use Ctrl+arrow keys to reduce the width of each cell to slightly larger than the header.

7. Press O for Options, P for Position ,C for Center, F7, F7. The entire table will be centered on the page.

8. Adjust title so it is flush with the upper left margin of the table.

9. Press Shift+F7 and V to view document and check table setup.

10. Press F7 to return to your text, leave three lines and resume typing.

SAVING

Every fifteen minutes you should save your paper to avert disaster.

1. Press F10 and the Save Dialog box appears. (Document to be saved prompt appears in **WordPerfect 4.2–5.1**).

2. Type a filename of no more than eight characters.

3. Press Enter. Your file name appears at lower left to show that it has been saved.

4. Every fifteen minutes, press Ctrl+F12 and your work will be saved to the disk. (Press F10, Enter and Y in **WordPerfect 4.2–5.1**).

Printing

1. Press Shift+F7 and the Print menu appears.

2. Press Enter. (Press 1 in WordPerfect 4.2–5.1).

3. Select from the Print menu for other options.

Footnote Citation with
Microsoft Word 5.0–6.0 for DOS

MARGINS

The setting for *Chicago Manual of Style* papers is one inch top, bottom and sides. The default setting for Microsoft Word is 1.25" left and right and 1.00" top and bottom. You need to adjust the left and right margins. Do not right justify or hyphenate.

Microsoft Word 6.0

1. Choose Margins from the Format Menu. The Section Margins dialog box appears.
2. Press L for Left and type 1".
3. Press R for Right and type 1".
4. Press U for Use as default and choose OK.

Microsoft Word 5.0

1. Press Esc, F for Format and D for Division.
2. Press M for Margins and Tab to move the highlight to the word, Left, and type 1".
3. Press Tab to move the highlight to the word, Right, and type 1".
4. Press Enter and Esc.
5. Press F, D, and L for Layout and Tab to division break.
6. Press spacebar to Continuous and press Enter.

LINE SPACING

Chicago Manual of Style papers are double spaced except for footnotes and bibliography entries which are single spaced.

Microsoft Word 6.0

1. Select the entire document by pressing Shift+F10.

2. Press Ctrl+2

3. Press Ctl+1 for single spacing.

Microsoft Word 5.0

1. Select the entire document by pressing Shift+F10.

2. Press Esc, F and P for Paragraph.

3. Press Tab to line spacing: 1 li.

4. Type 2 li and Enter.

5. Type 1 li and Enter to return to single spacing.

or

1. Press Alt+2 or Alt+1.

PAGINATION

Chicago Manual of Style papers are numbered consecutively in Arabic from first page of text to last page of bibliography at the top center of each page except for first pages of new sections such as bibliography and chapters which are numbered at the the bottom center of each page.

Preliminary pages such as the table of contents and dedication are numbered at the bottom center in small Roman numerals beginning with ii. because you count, but do not number the title page. The Table of Contents is usually numbered, ii.

Regular Pages

Microsoft Word 6.0

1. Choose Page Numbers from the Insert Menu. The Page Numbers dialog box appears.

2. Choose "From Top" in Page Number Position, "Center" in Align Page Number at, Arabic 1,2,3 in Format, the default option, "Auto," in Start at: and OK.

Microsoft Word 5.0

1. Press Esc, F, D, and P for Page-numbers.

2. Spacebar to Yes, Tab to "from left:" and type 4.25″.

3. Tab to "start numbering" and spacebar to Continuous.

4. Tab to at: and type 1. Tab to "number format" and select Arabic (1) and press Enter.

MICROSOFT DOS WORD

125

First Pages of New Sections

Paginating the first pages of new chapters and the preliminary pages presents a small problem. Solution: Print the entire paper beginning with the first page of text with all page numbers at the top. Pull out the first pages of new chapters or sections such as Bibliography.

Microsoft 6.0

1. Scroll to those pages and reformat them.
2. Move cursor to the last character on the page.
3. Choose Section from the Format Menu.
4. Choose Page Numbers. The Page Numbers dialog box will appear.
5. Choose "From Bottom" in Page Number Position and either Arabic or small Roman in Format as needed.
6. Choose Print from the File Menu.
7. Choose "Pages" from the Page Range drop down list.
8. Type the numbers of the pages you need to reprint with numbers at the bottom and print.

Remember to reformat these pages as before if you need to reprint your paper.

Microsoft Word 5.0

1. Scroll to those pages and reformat them.
2. Press Ctrl+Enter to start a new division.
3. Tab to "from top:" and type 10.5" to place page numbers at bottom.
4. Press Esc P for Print and O for Options.
5. Tab to "range:" and select (pages). Tab to "page numbers" and insert the page number of the page you reformatted.
6. Press Enter and Print.

Remember to reformat these pages as before if you need to reprint your paper.

PRELIMINARY PAGES

1. Follow above but select small Roman numbers.

INDENTION

Chicago Manual of Style papers are indented six to eight spaces. The

Microsoft Word default tab setting is one half inch. The correct tab setting will depend on the font used.

Microsoft Word 6.0

1. Press Shift+F10 to select whole document.
2. Choose Paragraph from the the Format Menu. The Paragraph dialog box appears.
3. Type new setting in tenths; e.g., 0.6 or 0.7 and choose OK.
4. Type ten test characters without a space and press Tab.
5. Count the number of characters in the new tab set.
6. Adjust as needed.

Microsoft Word 5.0

1. Press Esc, F, and Tab. The highlight appears on the word, Set.
2. Press Enter. (Left) will be in parenthesis with prompt, FORMAT TAB SET position.
3. Type new setting in tenths; e.g., .6, or .7, and press Enter.
4. Type ten test characters without a space and press Tab.
5. Count the number of characters in the new tab set.
6. Adjust as needed.

TITLE PAGE

1. Press Ctrl+Shift+Enter to start a new page.
2. Use your college or school style exactly. Otherwise, center and double space in all upper case: name of school, title of paper, your name, course, teacher's name, and date. The title page is not numbered.

FOOTNOTE CITATIONS

Microsoft Word will automatically number footnotes and place them at the bottom of each page.

Microsoft Word 6.0

1. Move the cursor immediately after the phrase or sentence you wish to cite without a space.
2. Choose Footnote from the Insert Menu. The Footnote dialog box appears with Auto-numbered Reference selected.

3. Choose OK. Press Tab to indent and type the footnote with no space between the footnote number and the footnote.

4. Use the appropriate format shown on pages 109–111 for the type of reference you are citing. The second and following lines begin at the margin. Single space within footnotes. Press Enter twice to double space between footnotes.

5. Leave the cursor within the footnote and press F5. The Go to dialog box appears.

6. Choose OK. The cursor will move back to the document.

7. Footnote numbers must appear as superscripts like this.[1] Move the cursor over the footnote numbers and press Shift+Ctrl+= (equal sign) to change numbers to superscript.

To Edit Footnotes:

1. Select the footnote number in the text and press F5. The Go to dialog box appears.

2. Choose OK and edit.

3. Press F5 and choose OK. The cursor will return to the document.

Microsoft Word 5.0

1. Move the cursor immediately after the phrase or sentence you wish to cite without a space.

2. Press Esc, F, and F for Footnote and Enter. Two diamonds appear with the number 1 for the first footnote between them. With the cursor over the number 1, use the spacebar or tab to indent the number six spaces.

3. Type the footnote with no space between the number and the footnote. Use the appropriate format shown on pages 109–111 for the type of reference you are citing. The second and following lines should begin at the margin. Single space within footnotes. Press Enter twice to double space between footnotes.

4. Press Esc J for Jump, F for Footnote when you finish typing the footnote. The cursor will move back to the document.

5. Footnotes numbers must appear as superscripts like this.[1] Move the cursor over the footnote numbers in the footnote and in the text and press Alt + +. Then use the arrow keys to resume typing.

To Edit Footnotes:

1. Select the footnote number in the text.
2. Press Esc, J, and F.
3. Edit the footnote and press J and F to return to text.

BIBLIOGRAPHY

1. Press Ctrl+Shift+Enter to start a new page.
2. Center the word, BIBLIOGRAPHY, in upper case thirteen lines from the top margin. Check the Command Area at the lower left of screen for the line number.
3. Double space twice and type entries in alphabetical order using the correct format shown on pages 112–114 for the type of reference you are citing.
4. First line of each entry begins at left margin with following lines single spaced and indented 6–8 spaces.
5. Double space between entries. The first page of the bibliography section is numbered at the bottom center.

TABLES

Microsoft Word 6.0

4. Choose Insert Table from the Table menu. The Insert Table dialog box appears.
5. Type in the number of columns (vertical) you need.
6. Type in the number of rows (horizontal) you need.
7. Press B to place lines around cells.
8. Choose OK and the table grid appears in your text.
9. Type headers at the top of each column and enter data in each cell using tab and arrow keys.
10. Center data and header titles in each cell using regular formatting.
11. Select Column Width from the Table menu. The dialog box appears.
12. Type the width in inches for each column as needed. Choose OK.
13. Center the table by selecting it and pressing Ctrl+C.
14. Double space and resume typing.

Microsoft Word 5.0

1. Move the cursor to the place in the text where the table will be inserted. Leave three blank lines.

2. Type at the margin Table 1.—And the Title Just Like This in upper and lower case and center. Extra lines are centered and single spaced.

3. Press O for Options, arrow to Yes for show ruler and Enter.

4. Press Esc, F, T for Tab, S for Set, and F1. A cursor appears on the ruler. Use arrow keys to move tabs to the locations for the columns.

5. Count the letters in the first header. If the first header title is the word, Subjects, the tab should be four spaces to the right of the T in Table.

6. Press C for Center alignment so data will be centered in the column.

7. Continue using arrow keys and pressing C at each stop estimating the space needed for each column and press Enter.

8. Type the headers. Press Shift+Enter twice at the end of each row. A small vertical arrow appears. This will start a new line, but keep the data in the same paragraph.

9. Enter the data using tabs. If you need to adjust the columns, high-light the table under the title.

10. Press Esc, F, T, S, and F1. Press Up or Down arrows to move to the tab you want to change.

11. Press Ctrl+Left or Right arrow to move tab stop and press Enter. Repeat for other stops.

12. Insert horizontal rules by using space bar to left margin of centered table and pressing hyphen key.

Footnote Citation with
WordPerfect for Windows 5.2–6.0

MARGINS

The setting for *Chicago Manual of Style* papers is one inch on top, bottom and sides. This is the WordPerfect default setting. You need to adjust the top margin to place the page numbers one half inch from the top on most pages and adjust the bottom margin to place the page number one half inch from the bottom for preliminary pages and first pages of chapters and new sections. Do not right justify or hyphenate.

For Top Numbers:

1. Click on Layout and Margins in the Menu Bar. The Margins dialog box appears. The Left box will be flashing.
2. Click on Top, press Delete and type in .5″.
3. Click on OK.

For Bottom Numbers:

1. Place the cursor on the page which needs a bottom number.
2. Click on Layout and Margins in the Menu Bar.
3. Click on Top, press Delete and type in 1″.
4. Click on Bottom, press Delete and type in .5″.

LINE SPACING

Chicago Manual of Style papers are double spaced except for footnotes and bibliography entries which are single spaced.

1. Click on Layout, Line and Spacing in the Menu Bar. The Line Spacing dialog box appears. The default setting is 1.
2. Click twice on the up arrow to change the setting to 2.
3. Click on OK.

or

1. Click on View and Ruler in the Button Bar. The Ruler appears.

2. Click on the last button on the right of the Button Bar.

3. Drag down to 2.0 lines and release.

PAGINATION

Chicago Manual of Style papers are numbered consecutively in Arabic from first page of text to last page of bibliography at the top center of each page except for first pages of new sections such as bibliography and chapters which are numbered at the the bottom center of each page.

Preliminary pages such as the table of contents and dedication are numbered at the bottom center in small Roman numerals beginning with ii. because you count, but do not number the title page. The Table of Contents is usually numbered, ii.

Regular Pages

1. Position the cursor on the first page of regular text and click on View and Ruler in the Menu Bar.

2. Click on Layout, Page and Headers in the Menu Bar. The Headers dialog box appears with Header A selected.

3. Click on Create. The header window appears with the cursor at the left margin.

4. Click on Page Number. A ^B symbol appears with the cursor following. Press Home to move the cursor to the left margin.

5. Press Shift F7 to center and click on OK.

First Pages of New Sections

1. Move the cursor to the page which needs a bottom number.

2. Click on Layout, Page and Headers in the Menu Bar.

3. Click on Edit. The ^B symbol appears. Select it and press Delete and Close.

4. Click on Layout, Page and Footers in the Menu Bar.

5. Click on Create and follow the directions for headers above.

Preliminary Pages

1. Follow the directions for First Pages of New Sections.

2. Click on Layout, Page and Numbering in the Menu Bar. The Page Numbering dialog box appears.

WORDPERFECT WINDOWS

3. Click on Number Types arrows and drag down to small Roman.

4. Click on OK.

INDENTION

Chicago Manual of Style papers are indented six to eight spaces. The Word-Perfect for Windows default setting is one half inch. The correct tab setting depends on the font used.

1. Type an unbroken line of 15 characters.

2. Press Tab and count the number of spaces at the default tab setting. If correct, leave the setting. If not:

3. Click on Layout, Line, and Tab Set in the Menu Bar. The Tab Set dialog box appears with default setting in the Relative Position box.

4. Click on Clear Tabs.

5. Try typing 0.7 in the Relative Position Box.

6. Click on Tab Set and OK. The tab will be set for .7″.

7. Press Tab and check the number of spaces at the new tab setting. Adjust as needed.

TITLE PAGE

1. Move cursor to the top of first page.

2. Use your college or school style exactly. Otherwise, center and double space in all upper case: name of school, title of paper, your name, course, teacher's name, and date. The title page is not numbered.

FOOTNOTE CITATIONS

WordPerfect for Windows will automatically number footnotes and place them at the bottom of each page.

1. Move the cursor immediately after the phrase or sentence you wish to cite without a space.

2. Click on Layout, Footnote, and Create in the Menu Bar. A footnote window and button bar appears with the number 1. at the left margin.

3. Type the footnote using the correct format shown on pages 109–111 for the type of reference you are citing.

4. Click on Close. The cursor will return to your text. When you create the next footnote, WordPerfect will automatically double space between footnotes.

To Edit a Footnote:

1. Click on Layout, Footnote and Edit in the Menu Bar. The Edit Foot-note dialog box appears.
2. Type the the number of the Footnote you want to edit.

To Delete a Footnote:

1. Select the footnote number of the footnote you want to delete in the text. Press Delete. All footnotes will be renumbered.

BIBLIOGRAPHY

1. Press Ctrl+Enter to start a new page.
2. Center the word, BIBLIOGRAPHY, in upper case thirteen lines down from the top margin.
3. Double space twice and type entries in alphabetical order using the appropriate correct format shown on page 112–114 for the type of reference you are citing.
4. First line of each entry begins at left margin with following lines single spaced and indented 6–8 spaces.
5. Double space between entries. The first page of the bibliography section is numbered at the bottom center.

TABLES

WordPerfect for Windows 5.2–6.0

1. Move the cursor to the place in the text where the table will be inserted. Leave three blank lines.
2. Type at the margin Table 1.—And the Title Just Like This in upper and lower case and center. Extra lines are centered and single spaced.
3. Click on View and Ruler in the Menu Bar. The Ruler will appear.
4. Click on the Table button in the ruler and drag down to the number of columns (vertical) and rows (horizontal) you want and release. The table appears spread across the screen.
5. Move the cursor from cell to cell with the arrow keys.
6. Enter the headers and data in each cell.
7. To adjust width of cells, drag the triangular markers above the ruler which separate the columns.

8. To center headers or data, select cells and click on the Justification button in the ruler. Drag down to Center and release.

9. To align decimal points, select the cells with decimal data, click on the Justification button in the ruler. Pull down to Decimal and release.

10. Move the entire table by clicking on Layout, Tables and Options. Click on Center in the Position box and click OK.

11. Select the entire table. Click on Layout, Tables and Lines. Select line styles as appropriate.

12. Click on File and Preview to check table setup.

Footnote Citation with
Microsoft Word for Windows 2.0–6.0

MARGINS

The setting for *Chicago Manual of Style* papers is one inch on top, bottom and sides. The default setting for Microsoft Word for Windows is 1.25" left and right and 1" top and bottom. You need to adjust left and right margins. Do not right justify or hyphenate.

1. Click on Format and Page Setup in the Menu Bar. The Page Setup dialog box appears.
2. Click on Margins on the top line. Move the cursor to Left and Right boxes with the mouse.
3. Click on the down arrows in the boxes until 1" appears.
4. Choose Whole Document or This Point Forward, whichever is appropriate, in the Apply to list.
5. Click on OK.

LINE SPACING

Chicago Manual of Style papers are double spaced except for footnotes and bibliography entries which are single spaced.

1. Place the cursor at the beginning of the document.
2. Press Ctrl+2.

PAGINATION

Chicago Manual of Style papers are numbered consecutively in Arabic from first page of text to last page of bibliography at the top center of each page except for first pages of new sections such as bibliography and chapters which are numbered at the the bottom center of each page.

Preliminary pages such as the table of contents and dedication are numbered at the bottom center in small Roman numerals beginning with ii. because you count, but do not number the title page. The Table of Contents is usually numbered, ii.

Microsoft Word for Windows 2.0–6.0

Regular Pages

1. Move the cursor to the first page of regular text.
2. Click on Insert and Page Numbers in the Menu Bar. The Page Numbers dialog box appears.
3. Choose Top of Page and Center.
4. Click on Format. The Page Number Format dialog box appears.
5. Choose Arabic numerals and OK. The Page Numbers dialog box reappears.
6. Click on OK.

First Pages of New Sections

1. Print the whole paper and pull out the pages which need bottom page numbers.
2. Scroll to each of the pages and repeat the process, but choose Bottom of Page. Reprint those pages separately.

Preliminary Pages

1. Type these pages separately as a separate section.
2. Repeat the process above, choosing Bottom of Page and Center.
3. Click on Format. The Page Number Format dialog box appears.
4. Choose small Roman numerals and OK. The Page Numbers dialog box reappears.
5. Click on OK.

INDENTION

Chicago Manual of Style papers are indented six to eight spaces. The Word for Windows default setting is one half inch. The correct tab setting will depend on the font used.

Microsoft Word For Windows 6.0

1. Click on View and Ruler in the Menu Bar. The ruler appears.
2. Click on the box at the left end of the ruler until the symbol L appears.
3. Type an unbroken series of at least 15 characters at the left margin.
4. Click inside the ruler where the sixth, seventh, or eighth character is located and release. The new first tab is set.

Microsoft Word For Windows 2.0

1. Click on View and Ruler in the Menu Bar. The ruler appears.
2. Type an unbroken series of at least 15 characters at the left margin.
3. Count 6, 7, or 8 characters as you desire.
4. Click on the tab marker at the .5" mark on the ruler and drag it to the sixth, seventh, or eighth character location and release. The new first tab is set.

TITLE PAGE

1. Move the cursor to the top line of the first page.
2. Use your college or school style exactly. Otherwise, center and double space in all upper case: name of school, title of paper, your name, course, teacher's name, and date. The title page is not numbered.

FOOTNOTE CITATIONS

Word for Windows will automatically number footnotes and place them at the bottom of each page.

Microsoft Word for Windows 2.0–6.0

1. Click on View and be sure you are in Normal View.
2. Move the cursor immediately after the phrase or sentence you wish to cite without a space.
3. Click on Insert and Footnote in the Menu Bar. The Footnote dialog box appears with Auto-Numbered Footnote selected.
4. Click OK. A footnote window appears. The number 1 will appear in superscript at the end of your text and at the left margin of the footnote window with the cursor just to the right.
5. Use the left arrow key to move the cursor to the left of the footnote number.
6. Press Tab to indent the first line of the footnote.
7. Move the cursor just to the right of the superscript number without a space.
8. Type the footnote using the appropriate format shown on pages 109–111 for the type of reference you are citing. Single space within the footnote and click on Close. The cursor will return to the main text.
9. Double space between footnotes and follow the same procedure for the next footnote.

To Edit a Footnote:

Microsoft Word for Windows 6.0

1. Double click on the footnote number in the text.
2. Edit the footnote and click on Close.

Microsoft Word for Windows 2.0

1. Press F5 twice. The Go to dialog box appears.
2. Type f space and the footnote number.
3. Edit the footnote and click on Close.

To Delete a Footnote:

Microsoft Word for Windows 6.0 and 2.0

1. Select the footnote number in the text and press Delete.

BIBLIOGRAPHY

1. Click on Insert and Break in the Menu Bar to start a new page. The Break dialog box appears with Page Break selected.
2. Double space and center the word, BIBLIOGRAPHY, in upper case. To check the position of the heading, click on File and Print Preview in the Menu Bar.
3. Double space twice and type entries in alphabetical order using the appropriate format shown on pages 112–114 for the type of reference you are citing. First line of each entry begins at left margin with following lines single spaced and indented six to eight spaces.
4. Double space between entries. The first page of the bibliography section is numbered at the bottom center.

TABLES

Microsoft Word for Windows 2.0 and 6.0

1. Move the cursor to the place in the text where the table will be inserted. Leave three blank lines.
2. Type at the margin Table 1--And the Title Just Like This in upper and lower case and center. Extra lines are centered and single spaced. Press Enter.

3. Click on the Insert Table button just above the B, I, U buttons in the upper toolbar. A table box appears.

4. Drag across the columns (vertical) and rows (horizontal) until you have the correct number of cells you need.

5. Move the cursor from cell to cell with the tab or arrow keys. Do not use Enter in the table.

6. Enter headers and data in each cell.

7. Click on Table in the Menu Bar and Select Table.

8. Click on Center button in the standard toolbar and all data in each cell will be centered.

9. Adjust the outside lines of the table by clicking on them. The cursor becomes two vertical lines with arrows pointing left and right. Drag the lines to the left and right edges of the table title.

10. Adjust the width of the columns by clicking on vertical lines and dragging them where you want them.

11. Move the cursor into the table and click on Table and and Center in the toolbar.